★★★★★★★★★★★★★★★★★★

BASEBALL
SUPERSTARS

Roger Maris

★★★★★★★★★★★★★★★★★★

Hank Aaron
Ty Cobb
Johnny Damon
Lou Gehrig
Rickey Henderson
Derek Jeter
Randy Johnson
Andruw Jones
Mickey Mantle
Roger Maris
Mike Piazza
Kirby Puckett
Albert Pujols
Mariano Rivera
Jackie Robinson
Babe Ruth
Curt Schilling
Ichiro Suzuki
Bernie Williams
Ted Williams

BASEBALL
SUPERSTARS

Roger
Maris

Anne M. Todd

CHELSEA HOUSE
PUBLISHERS
An imprint of Infobase Publishing

ROGER MARIS

Chelsea House
An imprint of Infobase Publishing
132 West 31st Street
New York NY 10001

Library of Congress Cataloging-in-Publication Data

Todd, Anne M.
  Roger Maris / Anne M. Todd.
    p. cm.— (Baseball superstars)
  Includes bibliographical references and index.
  ISBN 978-0-7910-9734-2 (hardcover)
  1. Maris, Roger, 1934-1985. 2. Baseball players—United States—Biography. 3. New York Yankees (Baseball team) I. Title. II. Series.
  GV865.M37T63 2008
  796.357092—dc22
  [B   2007029053

Series design by Erik Lindstrom
Cover design by Ben Peterson

Printed in the United States of America

Bang EJB 10 9 8 7 6 5 4 3 2 1

This book is printed on acid-free paper.

All links and Web addresses were checked and verified to be correct at the time of publication. Because of the dynamic nature of the Web, some addresses and links may have changed since publication and may no longer be valid.

✦ ✦ ✦ ✦ ✦ ✦ ✦ ✦ ✦ ✦ ✦ ✦ ✦ ✦ ✦ ✦

CONTENTS

Small-Town Upbringing

Roger Eugene Maras (he changed his name to Maris in 1955) was born on September 10, 1934, in Hibbing, Minnesota, a small mining town in the northeast region of the state. People once called Hibbing the "Iron Capital of the World" because of the large amounts of iron ore discovered there.

Roger's ancestors came to Hibbing in the early 1900s from Croatia, which is east of Italy across the Adriatic Sea. Around 1910, Roger's grandfather, Steve Maras, left Croatia for the United States. Once in Hibbing, Steve worked for his brother, who had already come from Croatia, at a saloon. Steve made a life for himself and his family, which included a son, Rudy. They lived on a settlement near one of the many mines. Rudy grew up and married Anne Corrine Sturbitz, who had been

Roger Maris relaxes on the dugout steps at Yankee Stadium. Maris played for the Yankees in bustling New York City from 1960 to 1966. His childhood years were spent far from the city—he was born on the Iron Range of Minnesota in a small town called Hibbing and later went to high school in Fargo, North Dakota.

raised in Calumet, Minnesota. The couple settled in Hibbing to raise a family.

Roger, who was the second son of Rudy and Anne Corrine Maras, was born in the middle of the Great Depression. Life on the Iron Range, as the area was known, was hard. Most people had little money, little food, and meager furnishings. Most everything in the town was tinted a rusty red because of the ever-present iron dust circulating in the air. Still, the Marases had much extended family in the area, and they all worked together to make their lives in the United States successful.

Rudy and Anne Corrine were Roman Catholics, as were most Croatians who immigrated to the United States. They instilled a strong work ethic in their two sons, Rudy Jr. (called Buddy) and Roger. They also created a loving family; Buddy and Roger learned to respect themselves and others.

The family worked hard, and they also played hard. Roger's father, Rudy, loved to participate in all kinds of sports. Before getting married, he had played baseball and hockey and had professional aspirations. In 1932, he had even tried out for the Boston Bruins of the National Hockey League, but he did not make the team. Rudy also played some semi-professional baseball. Although Rudy did not make a career out of sports, he passed his love of sports on to his children.

The harsh Minnesota winters and Hibbing's fairly remote northern location left little opportunity for any sports other than ice hockey. Young Roger and Buddy spent long hours playing ice hockey on the frozen ponds and lakes near their home. Hibbing was one of the first towns on the Iron Range to have an indoor hockey rink, so Roger and Buddy were able to play ice hockey all year. Rudy enjoyed watching his sons skate and seeing their athletic talents and competitive spirits begin to take shape.

ROGER'S YOUTH

In 1942, the family moved to Grand Forks, North Dakota, where they lived for two years. Rudy Maras had taken a job as a mechanical supervisor with the Great Northern Railroad. Anne Corrine Maras helped settle the family into their home, part of an eight-unit apartment building. Eight-year-old Roger easily made friends with the kids in the neighborhood and began school at Washington Elementary.

Buddy, who was a year older, and Roger became involved in school sports as soon as they were offered. Both boys had natural athletic abilities and enjoyed competition—between each other and against other teams. The brothers were close throughout their childhood; Roger considered Rudy Jr. to be his best friend. They enjoyed supporting each other, motivating each other, and helping each other reach their athletic goals.

At Washington Elementary School, Roger was co-captain of the basketball team. He also ran track and played football. The kids at Washington Elementary liked Roger, whom they described as a team leader. Roger played hard, and he played to win. Off the field, Roger was quiet yet headstrong. He took his responsibilities, like delivering newspapers around the neighborhood, seriously. He also enjoyed a good laugh and had fun goofing around with his friends.

When Roger was 10, the family moved to nearby Fargo, North Dakota, located along the Red River. The Marases immediately felt at home in Fargo; they liked the openness of the people and the attention and support their neighbors offered one another. They became affiliated with a Roman Catholic church and became close friends with Father John E. Moore. The Maras family found contentment in their routine of going to school and work during the week, playing on Saturdays, and attending church on Sundays.

Roger started the ninth grade in the fall of 1948, and he and his brother attended Fargo Central High School. During Roger's sophomore year, he met Patricia Ann Carvell, whom he would later marry. They met at a high school basketball game held in the gymnasium of St. Anthony of Padua Church. When Roger first spotted Pat on the opposite side of the gym,

☆ ☆ ☆ ☆ ☆
BREAKING BARRIERS: JACKIE ROBINSON

Jackie Robinson was born on January 31, 1919, in Cairo, Georgia. A year later, his mother moved his family to Pasadena, California, where Jackie was raised. At the University of California, Los Angeles, Robinson was a widely acclaimed star in football, baseball, basketball, and track. After he left UCLA, Robinson served in the United States Army for three years. In 1945, when Roger Maris was about 10 years old back in North Dakota, Robinson joined the Kansas City Monarchs of the Negro American League.

From the Negro Leagues, Robinson became the first African American to sign a contract with a major-league team—the Brooklyn Dodgers. He played one year in the minors and then started the 1947 season with the Dodgers; he won Rookie of the Year. In his first season, he had a league-leading 29 stolen bases, hit 12 home runs, and batted .297. In 1949, he was named the National League Most Valuable Player. Robinson played his entire 10-year career with the Dodgers. During his career, Robinson played in 1,382 games. He hit 137 home runs, with 734 RBIs and a lifetime .311 batting average.

After baseball, Robinson worked to improve the living conditions for black Americans. He became involved in the civil-rights movement in the 1950s and became friends with Dr. Martin Luther King Jr., the famed civil-rights leader. He was elected to the National Baseball Hall of Fame in 1962. Robinson died of a heart attack in 1972. To mark the fiftieth anniversary of the integration of the sport, Major League Baseball retired Robinson's number, 42, in 1997.

Jackie Robinson and Roger Maris share some baseball stories—possibly about those New York fans—during a benefit. In 1947, when Maris was still a youngster in North Dakota, Robinson became the first African-American player in the major leagues. He played for 10 seasons with the Brooklyn Dodgers.

he asked a teammate who she was. Roger and Pat were drawn to each other from the start. They greatly enjoyed each other's company and shared many of the same values and beliefs. Roger and Pat dated all through high school.

During the summer months throughout high school, Roger worked short-term jobs, including a stint as a delivery boy in a flower shop. Another summer, Roger worked at the railroad where his dad was employed. Roger loved to be outdoors. He loved the sunshine, the fresh air, and the feeling of freedom he felt while being outside. The physical labor involved in his job, such as pounding iron spikes, likely helped to develop strength in Roger's wrists and upper body. This power would later be a great asset to him as a baseball player.

Buddy dragged Roger along with him to baseball practice when Roger was not working or spending time with friends. At first, Roger did not want to go. Eventually, though, Roger came to want to play baseball even without his brother. In the summer of 1949, Roger played for the first time with the American Legion team in Fargo as an outfielder and a pitcher. Fourteen-year-old Roger batted left-handed and threw right-handed. He had a powerful swing and a precise aim.

Buddy and Roger came to be known as hitting threats around the American Legion league. Coaches on other teams would caution their pitchers about throwing anything good to the Maras brothers. The coaches told their pitchers to keep the pitches low or they were sure to see a ball hit out of the park.

FARGO'S SHANLEY HIGH SCHOOL

Toward the end of the 1949–1950 school year, Roger and Buddy transferred from Central High School to Shanley High. The brothers wanted to be starters on their teams, and they did not feel that Central was giving them the game time they deserved. Fargo's Shanley High School was named after Bishop John Shanley. It was a Catholic school run by the Presentation Order of Sisters. Roger made strong connections with the staff there and would continue to visit the sisters who taught at the school long after he graduated.

At this time, Roger especially loved football. Sid Cichy was Shanley High's football coach, as well as a history teacher. Cichy would later win a place in the National High School Athletic Coaches Association Hall of Fame. Although the brothers had arrived too late in the school year to play in the 1949–1950 season, Cichy was happy to have Roger and Buddy play football the following season. Buddy seemed to have potential as a professional athlete—be it football or baseball. And Roger was also a strong player—both offensively and defensively.

During the summer of 1950, Roger once again played baseball in the American Legion. His coach, Chuck Bentsen, watched the young batter hit home runs far out of the parks. Roger's batting average soared to .367, and his team won the North Dakota championship. His fellow players voted him the team's Most Valuable Player.

☆ ☆ ☆ ☆ ☆

AMERICAN LEGION

The American Legion baseball program, which began in 1925, is the oldest and largest nationwide baseball program in the United States. More than 10 million players (ages 15 to 19) have taken part in the program since it was established. Today, the American Legion also offers programs for younger athletes and programs designed specifically for girls. The goals of the American Legion are for young people to develop team discipline, individual character, leadership, and smart sportsmanship. The first national tournament was held in 1926, with 16 states represented.

Roger Maris played for the North Dakota American Legion in 1950 and 1951. He was voted the Most Valuable Player of his team in 1950. Maris became a member of the North Dakota American Legion Baseball Hall of Fame in 1977. This organization recognizes individuals from North Dakota who have participated in the American Legion baseball program and have gone on to excel in the field of baseball or other endeavors.

Roger was a junior and Buddy was a senior in the fall of 1950. Now that they were attending Shanley High at the start of the school year, they were able to take full advantage of all the sports it had to offer. Roger wasted no time. Roger and Buddy played football on the same team for Cichy. During one game, Roger was charging down the field with the football in his possession. When he glanced behind him, he saw his brother trailing the play. Roger immediately tossed the football to Buddy, who scored the touchdown. Roger's generous character was emerging.

The Maras brothers both made the Associated Press East-West High School Football Team after Shanley High School won the eastern division title. They particularly enjoyed playing together against their former school, Fargo Central High. During that game, Roger scored two touchdowns off passes from Buddy. The brothers looked forward to teaming up again for the championship game, but a blizzard canceled the contest. As the school year wound down, Roger participated in other sports at Shanley, like track and basketball. When Buddy graduated in June 1951, Roger was saddened to see his school years with his brother end.

SENIOR YEAR

The 1951–1952 school year was Roger's senior year of high school. It was a year filled with good memories and special activities for seniors. One such happy occasion was when Roger took Pat to the senior prom. Roger picked her up for the dance in his father's 1932 Chevrolet.

Roger valued friendship and stayed in touch with many of his high school friends throughout his adult life. He treated his friends like family. Among his close friends, Roger could show the humorous side of his personality, and he enjoyed sharing laughs with them. Once, for instance, he and his friends filled the nuns' overshoes with flour without them knowing.

Roger's senior year, though, also had its challenges, including keeping up with academics. Roger was not a poor student, although his mind did not always stay focused on his studies. Still, he was determined to keep his grades up to be able to participate in sports. Roger knew the importance of good grades, though his own grades remained average throughout his schooling. He sometimes came in before school and stayed afterward to get extra help in the subjects that were more difficult for him, like geometry. His teachers enjoyed having him in class because he was responsible and respectful.

Although the people in Fargo knew Roger best for his abilities in football, he also excelled at other sports. In basketball, Roger was especially good on defense because he was so quick on his feet. He often stole the ball and ran to the other end of the court for an easy lay-up. In track, Roger competed in dashes, relays, the shot put, and the long jump. He placed second in the 100-yard dash and third in the shot put at the North Dakota State Class A Championships.

In baseball, Roger nearly always swung on the first pitch, as he had an intense desire to hit the ball. He thought it was dishonorable to get on base with a walk instead of a hit. Leo Osman was Roger's American Legion coach in 1951. Osman thought that Roger's timing was right on. He could see that Roger knew when and where to hit. Roger was quick and strong. The strength in his wrists and upper body were essential to making a good baseball player.

In football, Roger was strong on offense and defense. He was able to run, block, and catch the ball easily; he could also intercept passes and tackle. Coaches enjoyed working with him because he listened and responded to advice. Roger was extremely dedicated to any sport in which he participated. He missed only one football practice during his two years on Cichy's team.

During a football game against Devil's Lake, Roger scored four touchdowns on kickoff returns. His numbers set a national

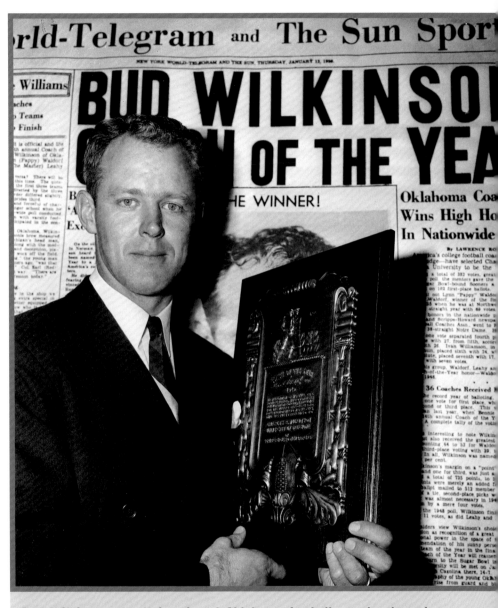

Bud Wilkinson, the University of Oklahoma football coach, showed off his 1949 Coach of the Year plaque during the American Football Coaches Association dinner. In 1952, Wilkinson offered Roger Maris a scholarship to play football at Oklahoma. It was a tossup whether Roger would try to pursue his athletic dreams on the football field or the baseball diamond.

high school record. Cichy saw that Roger was a truly gifted athlete. It was no surprise to Cichy or anyone else in Fargo when Bud Wilkinson, the famed coach from the University of Oklahoma, offered Roger a scholarship to play in his football program. Wilkinson, whose real name was Charles Burnham Wilkinson, started to coach at the University of Oklahoma in 1947. In his first season, he guided his team to a 7–2–1 record and the Big Six championship. The team won the title again in '48, '49, and '50. Wilkinson offered Roger room and board in addition to tuition. Roger had a lot of thinking to do and a major decision to make.

The Early
Baseball Years

Roger Maras graduated from high school in June 1952. He had worked hard to ensure that he finished with fairly good grades; he understood the importance of education and knew he could not merely rely on his athletic abilities to get him through life. He had offers from the University of Oklahoma and other colleges to play football at their schools. After talking with his family and thinking about his choices, Roger decided to give Oklahoma a closer look. It felt like the best option for him. Indeed, it was looking as if his passion for football would evolve into a career. Roger packed up his bags and went to visit the university.

At Oklahoma, Roger walked around the campus, met some professors, and took exams that would qualify him for the athletic program. During the exams, Roger struggled with doubt as he filled in his answer sheet. Although he thought that college would benefit him in the end, he also felt it was not where he wanted to be at the time. He worried that college life was not for him. He liked to be outdoors and moving around—not cooped up and sitting at a desk. Roger returned to Fargo, ready to rethink his choices.

Around this time, Buddy Maras became sick with polio, a highly infectious disease caused by a virus that invades the nervous system. In mere hours, it can cause total paralysis. In the 1940s and the 1950s, polio epidemics spread fear and panic across the United States. Polio forced Buddy to give up any plans for professional sports. Roger later said that, if his brother had been able to play football in college, he, too, would have continued with football. With his brother sick, however, Roger decided that what he really wanted to do was stay in Fargo. He felt a strong bond with his family and was not ready to leave.

FROM FOOTBALL TO BASEBALL

Roger decided to set his sights on baseball. Playing baseball would allow him everything he wanted: being outdoors, playing a sport, and remaining in Fargo for a while. Once Roger had made his decision, all he could do was continue to play for the city teams and wait for someone to discover him. Today, hundreds of well-trained scouts travel all over the country to find young talent. In the 1950s, such scouting was just beginning, mostly concentrated in large metropolitan areas.

Nonetheless, Frank Fahey, a part-time scout for the Cleveland Indians, had attended the 1950 American Legion tournament. He had seen Roger Maras play. Frank had noted in his files at that time that Roger already had impressive strength and, once he put on some weight, might be a good prospect to play professional baseball. Now that Roger had graduated from high school, Fahey asked him to come to Cleveland's tryout camp. Fahey wanted to see if Roger's abilities fit the needs of the team. Roger agreed. Hank Greenberg, the Cleveland Indians' general manager, was there to watch, too. The Indians liked Roger's home-run power.

After Roger returned home, Greenberg sent a representative to Fargo to sign Roger to the team. Other teams had heard about Roger, too, and came around to talk to him. Roger and his father worried about Roger playing baseball straight from high school. Would he benefit from playing college baseball first? College baseball would help take Roger to the next level of play. It would give him a broader knowledge of baseball. At the same time, he could earn a degree so that he would have something to fall back on if a baseball career did not work out. If he did not play college baseball, would Roger make it to the majors or would he be destined to remain in the minors?

After much talk and negotiations, the Maras family and the Indians came to an agreement. In 1953, 18-year-old Roger signed a contract for $15,000 with the Cleveland Indians of the American League. If he made it to the major leagues, the Indians would give Roger a bonus of $10,000. Roger Maras's baseball career had begun.

Roger started out in the minor leagues in 1953 and would play there for four years. He traveled from his hometown to Daytona Beach, Florida, where he began spring training. The organization was looking to place Roger with its farm team in Daytona, which was in a Class D League.

Roger, however, was not ready to leave his family and friends for an extended period. He let the Cleveland Indians know that he wanted to play close to home and was able to persuade them to let him play for the Fargo-Moorhead Twins in the Class C Northern League. This feat was not an easy one for two reasons: First, managers did not want their boys to play in their hometowns, as it often brought the young players unneeded pressures and distractions. Second, Roger better fit with the players in the Class D league in terms of his age; he

Back when he was an outfielder with the Detroit Tigers, Hank Greenberg had to haul away a load of fruit, vegetables, and other items that were thrown at the Tigers by Indian fans at Cleveland Stadium during a September 1940 game. In the 1950s, Greenberg was no longer an opponent of the Indians—he was the team's general manager. In that position, he signed a young Roger Maris to the organization.

would be a year younger than most of the others playing in a Class C league.

LIFE IN THE MINORS

Nonetheless, Roger believed that he was ready for Class C and would not back down. His insistence paid off. The Indians sent Roger to the Fargo-Moorhead Twins under manager Zeke Bonura. Bonura had Roger batting seventh in the starting lineup. On opening night, Roger had one hit in three at-bats. Despite Roger's quiet game, the Twins defeated Sioux Falls 12-3. Roger worked hard in practice and on his own to improve his swing, keep in shape, and step up his overall game. His hard work and dedication to improvement yielded results. He brought his batting average up to .329 and helped to lead the Fargo-Moorhead Twins to the 1953 Northern League championship. Roger earned the George Treadwell-Duluth Dukes Memorial Award as the Northern League's Rookie of the Year.

Although Roger spent much of his time working on his game, his life did not revolve around baseball. When not on the field, Roger was a courteous, responsible young man. He was a person of steadfast beliefs with an open and honest personality. He had a strong connection to his Roman Catholic faith. He felt a loyalty to Fargo and strived to be a good citizen and member of the community.

Roger's popularity and growing fame throughout North Dakota did not cause him to become arrogant. On the contrary, Roger was humble at heart. After winning a game, he avoided making a showy fuss and declined to celebrate excessively. He preferred quiet, low-key get-togethers out of the spotlight with his girlfriend, Pat Carvell, and other close friends. He liked to keep his private life private and was not interested in the public watching his every move.

Roger continued to take on odd jobs, pumping gas or making deliveries, when not playing ball. He also dedicated a portion of his time to others. From a young age, Roger had felt a strong desire to help people in need. Throughout his life, Roger would spend time visiting hospitals and making donations to various charities. He believed in anonymous charity work and did not like to talk about the money he gave away—he even asked close friends and family to keep his generosity secret. He did not think it right to share his charitable actions with the newspapers. He was clear that he was not donating his time and money to gain popularity; he was giving to help those in need. Roger needed no recognition for that. As he became more famous, he had more money to share.

At 18, Roger visited an orphanage associated with his high school to interact with the orphans—throwing a football around with them, chatting, and having fun. He wanted to help these kids, who were living in unusual circumstances, experience some normal activities. Roger made a point of treating people the way he would want to be treated.

MOVING THROUGH THE MINORS

In 1954, Roger, ready to move up the minor-league ranks to a Class B league, knew it was time to say good-bye to Fargo. Although it was hard to leave his longtime girlfriend, Pat, he was ready to take the step that would lead him toward his goal of playing in the majors. The Cleveland Indians had a Class B farm team in Keokuk, Iowa, in the Three-I League.

Roger started the 1954 season with the Keokuk Kernels, under manager Jo-Jo White. White had spent most of his major-league career playing for the Detroit Tigers. Like Roger, he was a left-handed batter and right-handed thrower. He was a great mentor to Roger, and Roger was receptive to White's advice. White taught Roger how to be a pull hitter, or someone who generally hits to the same side of the field as he bats. For example, Roger, being a left-handed batter, would try to pull the ball right down the line along the right edge of the field (as opposed to hitting the ball straight out into center field or away from himself into left field). By mastering this skill, Roger increased his power, hitting 32 home runs.

☆ ☆ ☆ ☆ ☆ ☆

MINOR LEAGUE BASEBALL

Minor League Baseball acts as an umbrella organization for the smaller minor leagues in North America. When it formed in 1901, the group was called the National Association of Professional Baseball Leagues (NAPBL). The following leagues were the first to join the NAPBL: Eastern League, Western League, New England League, New York State League, Pacific Northwest League, Southern Association, Three-I League, Carolina League, Connecticut League, Cotton States League, Iowa-South Dakota League, Michigan State League, Missouri Valley League, and the Texas League.

In 1949, with World War II won and Americans packing into ballparks to watch baseball, the number of leagues reached its peak at 59. That year, nearly 39.7 million fans attended minor-league games, a record that would last for 54 years. Over the course of the next few decades, attendance would decline, mainly because of the increase of televised major-league games. Today, there are 20 leagues under the Minor League Baseball organization.

When young players are signed by major-league teams, they are usually sent to the minor leagues to improve until they are ready to play in the majors. Until 1963, the minor leagues, also called the farm system, were broken down into these classes: Class D, Class C, Class B, Class A, Class AA, and Class AAA. After 1963, minor-league teams were divided into Rookie, Class A, Class AA, and Class AAA. Managers pull players from Class AAA to play in the major leagues.

Besides his hitting, Roger continued to impress people with his speed (he stole a base nearly every night) and fielding (he attacked every play in the outfield without holding back). Once during a home game, Roger ran through a wooden fence while chasing a fly ball. Roger was an aggressive player. He saw injury as a part of baseball and did not worry about what could happen to his body during a play. "Just because I get hurt is no reason to stop hustling. I'd rather stop playing than hustling," Maris said, as related in *Still a Legend: The Story of Roger Maris.* Despite smashing through the fence, Roger ended up with the ball in his glove. He was happy to have made the out and help his team. The Keokuk Kernels ended the 1954 season in second place in the Three-I League with a 78–58 record.

Because of Roger's continued improvement, the Cleveland Indians moved Roger up to Class AA, where he began the 1955 season in Tulsa, Oklahoma; after a brief time there (he played in only 25 games), Roger moved over to Reading, Pennsylvania, in the Eastern League to finish out the season.

Roger did not get along with manager Dutch Meyer when he arrived in Tulsa. Meyer worried about starting Roger because he was inexperienced, so Roger found himself sitting on the bench much of the time. Tension between Meyer and Roger was thick. When Roger continued to see little time on the field, he requested a transfer.

While in Reading in 1955, Roger again had the opportunity to work under manager Jo-Jo White, who had moved over from Keokuk to coach in Reading. Roger's game quickly improved after joining the Reading lineup. Once again, Roger learned a great deal more about the game of baseball from White. Roger was still young and inexperienced; White was able to help Roger grow as a person and a player. Roger led the Reading Indians in home runs, RBIs, walks, stolen bases (tied with teammate Lawrence Raines), and sacrifice flies. It was during this year, in 1955, that Roger Maras officially changed

Jo-Jo White had some fun riding a bike around the bases at Navin Field in Detroit in 1934. White was the manager of two minor-league teams that Roger Maris played for in the Cleveland Indians farm system. White helped Maris to grow as a player and as a person.

his last name from Maras to Maris. The change in spelling would help to avoid mispronunciations when fans yelled his name from the stands.

Between seasons, Roger returned to Fargo. When Roger traveled around the United States during the 1950s, he could sense the country's state of unrest. Inequalities between African Americans and whites were striking. Segregation of whites and blacks occurred in schools, restaurants, and on buses. In December 1955, an African-American woman named Rosa Parks boarded a bus in Montgomery, Alabama. She sat down on a seat near the front of the bus. When the driver asked Parks to give up her seat to a white man, she refused. Parks was arrested. Her decision to remain in her seat led to the beginning of the civil-rights movement. A man named Martin Luther King Jr. would lead a boycott of the bus system in Montgomery the following year.

In 1956, Roger played in Indianapolis, Indiana, in the Class AAA American Association, one rung below the major leagues. Roger struggled at the beginning of the 1956 season, and manager Kerby Farrell had no choice but to sit him on the bench. Roger met with him to say that he could not improve while sitting on the bench, that he needed to be in the lineup. Farrell agreed to let him play regularly for a 10-day trial. If Roger could turn his hitting around, Farrell would keep him in the lineup. If he failed, Farrell would pull him again. Roger delivered. By the end of the 1956 season, Roger had a batting average of .293, with 17 home runs and 75 RBIs, and he helped get the team to the Little World Series championships. The Little World Series featured the top teams in the American Association and the International League, among the best minor-league circuits at the time. In 1956, Indianapolis defeated Rochester of the International League, four games to none. Farrell won the *Sporting News* Minor League Manager of the Year award at the end of the season.

Roger's improvement in batting and fielding over the course of 1956 greatly impressed both Farrell and Cleveland Indians general manager Hank Greenberg. Roger had also shown maturity and a respect for the game of baseball that was apparent to managers and teammates alike. Farrell and Greenberg liked what they saw in this rising star, whom the fans had started calling "Cleveland's future Mickey Mantle." Clearly, Roger was going to get that $10,000 bonus after all—he was headed for the majors.

From the Minors to the Majors

Roger Maris, by now 22, married his high school sweetheart, Pat, who was one year younger, on October 13, 1956. They were married at St. Anthony of Padua Church, where Roger had first seen Pat during a basketball game. The wedding was a small, private ceremony with family and friends. Having gone to high school with Roger and then watching him make his way through the minor leagues, Pat knew firsthand what a baseball schedule was like. She knew that Roger would have to be away for days, weeks, and even months at a time. Like Roger, though, Pat was strong, courageous, and self-reliant. She and Roger made a good team. The couple eventually had six children—Susan, Roger Jr., Kevin, Randy, Richard, and Sandra.

During the first years of marriage, travel did force Roger to leave Pat alone for long periods during the regular season. Although they missed each other, they were determined to make their family work. Their strength and determination got them through their loneliness, and a solid marriage resulted.

MAJOR LEAGUER

Newlywed Roger Maris left Pat in Fargo in early 1957 and headed to Tucson, Arizona. Here, he began spring-training camp with the Cleveland Indians to prepare for the 1957 season. Spring training has been around almost as long as baseball; by 1900, it was an established part of the major leagues. Players have the opportunity to meet new teammates, practice together, run drills, and play in exhibition games. Spring training usually lasts two months, beginning in February and running through March. Managers have a chance to decide on their rosters and lineup (batting order).

Kerby Farrell had just become the Indians' new manager, so Maris was playing under someone he knew and respected. Training camp went well for Maris, and he felt ready to play in the big leagues. It was time to make Ohio home.

Roger and Pat Maris were in for a lot of change as he shifted from the minors to the majors. In the minors, Maris spent years traveling and moving from one league to another. Now, Roger and Pat could finally be together—at least some of the time. They rented a house in Parma, Ohio. Just 15 minutes from Cleveland, the move allowed Roger to live at home with Pat during the season when he was in town for home games. During his rookie year with the Indians, the couple's first child, Susan, was born while Roger was away at a road game.

Maris's career with the Cleveland Indians started out strong. On Opening Day, April 16, 1957, Roger went 3-for-5 against the Chicago White Sox. On day two of his major-league

After four years on five teams in the minor leagues, Roger Maris made it to the majors—and the Cleveland Indians—in 1957. He got off to a blistering start, but then injuries placed him on the disabled list twice. Maris had a difficult time regaining his form for the rest of the season.

career, Maris hit a grand slam, winning the game in the top of the eleventh inning. After 16 games, he had a .312 batting average. People were buzzing about Maris's hitting abilities and his impressive defensive moves in the outfield. He could throw balls from his position in right field to home plate to keep an opponent from scoring a run.

People grew to recognize Maris from his blond crew cut, strong facial features, and muscular build. His blue eyes narrowed when he stepped up to the plate and concentrated on the pitch. His 6-foot, 204-pound (183-centimeter, 92.5-kilogram) frame could feel daunting to an infielder when Maris came sliding thunderously into a base.

One month into the season, Maris's aggressive base running led to some injuries. First, he slid into second base and caught the knee of the second baseman in his side. Maris continued to play for two innings after the accident; he finally sat out the remainder of the game when he found he could not properly swing the bat. Upon examination, doctors found that Maris had broken two ribs. He was placed on the disabled list for a month. Less than a month after his return, he was back on the disabled list because of problems with his right foot.

Maris had had a good beginning to his season and also hit well between his periods on the disabled list. He had a hard time, though, returning to form after being on the disabled list the second time. Maris finished his first year in the majors with 14 home runs, 51 RBIs, and a .235 batting average.

NEED FOR A FRESH START

With a disappointing end to his first year in the majors, Maris was ready for the off-season and the family time it would bring. He, Pat, and Susan moved back to Fargo for the off-season, spending happy days together and catching up with old friends. Maris took a job as an account executive for the KVOX radio station.

Frank Lane took over for Hank Greenberg as the general manager of the Cleveland Indians during the off-season. Lane and Maris did not get along from the start. Lane had his own ideas about how Maris would spend his off-season. He ordered Maris to play in the winter league in the Dominican Republic.

★ ★ ★ ★ ★ ★

SMOKING—THEN AND NOW

Throughout Roger Maris's baseball career, he would endure many physical injuries. Maris's aggressive base running and fielding left him prone to getting hurt. What would end up hurting Maris the most, however, happened off the field—not on. Maris was a three-pack-a-day cigarette smoker. Although he did quit smoking in the 1970s, his 20-year habit would have serious effects.

Maris grew up at a time when smoking cigarettes was common and the public did not realize the deadly consequences. By the early 1960s, tobacco companies knew that nicotine was addictive, but to the public, they declared it was not. The tobacco industry also tried to cast doubt over any scientific evidence that proved that smoking was bad for a person's health. It was not until 1982 that the Surgeon General's Report stated: "Cigarette smoking is the major single cause of cancer mortality in the United States." That remains true today. Cigarette smoking accounts for at least 30 percent of all cancer deaths.

After Maris's death, the MeritCenter in Fargo, North Dakota, opened the Roger Maris Cancer Center. The center, which was established in 1990, is a major regional treatment center for cancer patients. It provides medical care, chemotherapy, and radiation therapy. The Roger Maris Celebrity Benefit Golf Tournament donates a part of its earnings each year to the Roger Maris Cancer Center.

He planned to move Maris from right field to center field, and he thought Maris could begin to work at this new position by playing winter ball. Maris refused; he did not intend to take time away from Pat and Susan. His family came first. Maris's decision angered Lane, who felt that Maris had his priorities mixed up.

The 1958 season brought other changes, as well. Bobby Bragan was the new manager for the Cleveland Indians. Bragan and Maris did not get along, either. The dislike between the two men affected Maris's game. He was not playing well, and it looked as if a trade was likely. That trade became a reality on June 15, 1958. The Indians traded Maris, pitcher Dick Tomanek, and infielder Preston Ward to the Kansas City Athletics of the American League for first baseman Vic Power and infielder Woodie Held. In Maris's abbreviated season with the Indians, he had hit 9 home runs and driven in 27 RBIs in 51 games. His batting average was .225. His numbers for the rest of the 1958 season in Kansas City improved somewhat. In 99 games, he hit .247 with 19 home runs and 53 RBIs.

The trade to Kansas City meant yet another move for Pat and the children, too. The growing family now included a new baby, Roger Jr. It was not hard, however, to move away from Ohio and the disappointing memories it held. The young family looked forward to a fresh start; they liked Missouri right away and felt at home there. They liked it so much so, in fact, that they decided to buy a house instead of renting one. They found a house and neighborhood they liked in nearby Raytown.

Maris made lasting friendships with his teammates from Kansas City. One such friend was Bob Cerv, an outfielder for the Athletics. Cerv was eight years older than Maris, so he was like an older brother to him. Both men came from small towns, enjoyed hunting in their spare time, and valued family. Like Maris, Cerv also lived close to the ballpark, so they spent time together in the off-season as well as during the regular season.

The Cleveland Indians got a new general manager and a new manager after the 1957 season, and Roger Maris did not get along well with either man. In June 1958, the Indians traded Maris to the Kansas City Athletics. Pat and Roger Maris felt at home right away in Missouri.

Maris felt that he was in good shape entering spring training for the 1959 season. He was comfortable with his new Kansas City club. In turn, the Athletics liked Maris's speed, power hitting, and defensive skills in the outfield. By mid-May, his batting average was an impressive .339, and he had 26 RBIs and 10 home runs.

Kansas City's manager, Harry Craft, had respect for the young ballplayer. Maris's early numbers earned him a spot on the American League All-Star team. In 1959, the major leagues held two All-Star Games, and Maris played in the game on August 3 in Los Angeles, California.

Earlier in the season, near the end of May, however, Maris had an emergency appendectomy. The operation left Maris in a slump that took him a long time to shake. On the days that Maris had bad games, Craft would sit down with him and talk about how certain plays could have gone differently. Maris appreciated Craft's willingness to teach and offer suggestions instead of simply getting frustrated and angry, as some managers did. Through the end of the season, Maris continued to come out of his slump: He ended the 1959 season with a .273 batting average, 72 RBIs, and 16 home runs.

MARIS IN PINSTRIPES

Maris had now played three years in the majors. During the off-season, on December 11, 1959, the New York Yankees of the American League negotiated a deal with the Kansas City Athletics. Maris was not part of these negotiations. In fact, Maris heard through the media, along with everyone else, about the transaction: Maris, infielder Joe DeMaestri, and first baseman Kent Hadley would become New York Yankees in exchange for pitcher Don Larsen, outfielder Hank Bauer, first baseman/outfielder Marv Throneberry, and first baseman/outfielder Norm Siebern.

Roger and Pat Maris were sad to learn about the trade, because they had come to think of Missouri as their home.

They liked the small size of the city; Maris worried that he would not like living in a city the size of New York. Pat was now expecting their third child, as well. The couple did not want her to move away from her doctor in the middle of her pregnancy. Pat, Susan, and Roger Jr. would stay in Raytown, Missouri. The family would be split apart once more.

Although reluctant to leave his family, Maris appeared in St. Petersburg, Florida, ready for spring training with the Yankees. He would play hard and stay focused no matter what city he played in; Roger Maris simply wanted to play baseball. The Yankees, led by manager Casey Stengel, tried Maris in left field during spring training, but they decided he played better in right field. Maris would begin the season there.

The time had come to face the big city. One person who knew that this change could be overwhelming to Maris was his former teammate Bob Cerv. Cerv asked Julius "Big Julie" Isaacson, the president of the Novelty Workers Union and a friend of Cerv's, to meet Maris at the airport and help to get him settled. Isaacson agreed.

When the 25-year-old Maris appeared at the airport, he wore corduroy jeans and a sweater with white buckskin shoes. Isaacson, wanting to help him fit into his new surroundings, told Maris that the Yankees did not dress like that—they wore jackets and ties. Maris replied that he would go back to Kansas City if the Yankees did not like how he dressed. Maris was not about to change his style to "fit in" with New Yorkers. Isaacson liked Maris's honesty and willingness to stand by his beliefs; in fact, Isaacson shared these very traits himself. The two, although from quite different backgrounds, hit it off, and they became lifelong friends.

Maris, of course, had no place to live in New York. He stayed briefly in a few hotels in Manhattan but decided he did not like Manhattan, which is one of five boroughs in New York City. Isaacson helped Maris by renting him an apartment in Queens, another borough of New York City. Then, in May

By the 1960 season, Roger Maris was on the move again—this time, he was donning the famous pinstripes of the New York Yankees. He was joining a team with a rich history in a city known for its media glare.

1960, Bob Cerv arrived in New York after the Athletics traded him to the Yankees, too. Once again, Maris and Cerv would be playing on the same team. Soon after, the two friends decided to become roommates, sharing the Queens apartment. With their similar lifestyles and interests, they were a good match.

Maris was ready to don the Yankees' widely recognized white uniform with black pinstripes. The pinstripes on the uniforms had made their debut in 1912. Maris's wool uniform, with the overlapping "N" and "Y" off to one side, would display the number 9 on the back. He may not have felt comfortable in the crowded, noisy city of New York, but when Maris stepped onto the Merion bluegrass of Yankee Stadium's field in the Bronx, he felt right at home. The gigantic, horseshoe-shaped ballpark had three tiers of seating and a roof extending over part of the third tier. The stadium had opened in April 1923 and was nicknamed "The House That Ruth Built" after Yankee legend Babe Ruth. In this house, Roger Maris was about to begin his New York Yankee career.

YANKEE LIFE

Maris was joining a team known for its rich history and baseball greats. When Maris joined the New York Yankees in 1960, the club included baseball stars Elston Howard (catcher), Bill Skowron (first base), Bobby Richardson (second base), Clete Boyer (third base), Tony Kubek (shortstop), Héctor López (left field), Mickey Mantle (center field), and Yogi Berra (catcher and outfielder). Maris would now be a part of this roster in right field.

The New York Yankees were used to being in the spotlight. The media spent a great deal of time writing about Mantle, who was a fan favorite in New York. Mantle had not always had a good rapport with the press. There was a time when reporters criticized his high number of strikeouts, ridiculed him for being injury-prone, and accused him of being a "hick" from Oklahoma. Over time, though, Mantle learned what the reporters wanted to see and hear, and he delivered. He also became known for his powerful hitting—especially his ability to knock out home runs that traveled 500 feet (152 meters) or more. In addition, he was known for living it up—attending parties, staying out late drinking and dancing—and he seemed to have a great time doing it. To the fans and to the media, Mantle epitomized a person living the American Dream.

The press did not quite know what to make of newcomer Roger Maris, who dressed a little differently from the other players. His home runs were nothing spectacular—generally less than 400 feet (122 meters). Then, too, there was the fact that Maris talked openly about not liking the big city. Reporters also found that Maris was hard to interview because he preferred not to discuss his private life. So no matter how many different ways a reporter asked a particular question, Maris often replied with answers that left reporters unsatisfied and wanting more.

Some reporters described Maris, just as they had Mantle, as a small-town hick. Others referred to him as sulky. Maris quickly realized that sportswriters did not always report exactly what they heard. Sometimes they would leave out parts of what Maris said, changing the meaning. Other times they would misinterpret what he had said entirely. And in still other instances, they would simply lie. Maris recognized early in his Yankee days that the New York press could turn out to be a problem for him.

The MVP Years

Reporters aside, the 1960 season started strong for Roger Maris and the Yankees. In Maris's first game on April 19, he hit a single, a double, and two home runs against the Red Sox at Fenway Park. As the season got under way, not only was Maris's hitting consistent, but his fielding was also helping the Yankees win games. Opponents soon learned to be conservative on the base paths. When a runner tried to turn that final corner to score a run, Maris was sure to throw him out at the plate from deep right field. Maris's throws were strong and accurate—he became a huge asset to the Yankees.

Halfway through his first year with the Yankees, Maris led the major leagues with 27 home runs and 69 RBIs. He made the American League All-Star team. Two All-Star Games continued to be played in 1960, with the first on July 11 at Municipal

Stadium in Kansas City, Missouri, and the second on July 13 at Yankee Stadium in New York. The National League won both games.

Maris's growing success on the field brought an onslaught of reporters. Maris was still wary and uncomfortable around them. He would have preferred to go straight back to his apartment after a game, not face flashbulbs and microphones and notepads. Lately, as his home-run total mounted, the reporters seemed to have only one question on their minds: "Do you think you have a chance of beating Babe Ruth's home-run record?" Maris's standard response was that he was not interested in breaking the record—he just wanted to have a good year and see the Yankees win the pennant.

1960 PENNANT RACE

Back in New York after the All-Star break, the race for the American League pennant was close. The Yankees were battling with the Baltimore Orioles and the Chicago White Sox to win the American League title. Whichever team ended the season with the best record would face the National League champion in the World Series.

In one critical game, with a runner on base, Gene Freese of the Chicago White Sox hit a ball fast and deep into center field—it looked as if Freese would be able to get to third base and the runner on base was sure to score. Unfortunately, Mickey Mantle could not reach the ball in time. But then, Maris came racing over from right field and caught the ball, stopping the triple and saving a run. The Yankees went on to win the game. Many reporters at the time pointed to this catch as the play that most helped the Yankees get to the World Series.

Unfortunately, Maris's unyielding base-running style caused him another injury in August. Running the bases in a game against the Washington Senators, Maris collided with Billy Gardner at second. In the collision, Maris ripped a muscle in his side. The Yankees put Maris on the disabled list. After missing 17 games, he was able to return before Labor Day and finish out the year. While on the disabled list, he was happy to learn of the birth of his third child, Kevin.

Maris's 1960 season was highly successful for him. He played in 136 games, with a batting average of .283, 39 home runs (second in the league), and 112 RBIs (first in the league). Mantle led the league in home runs, with 40. Maris joined the Yankees in competing in his first World Series in October 1960. The Yankees were up against the Pittsburgh Pirates. Maris hit two home runs during the seven-game series, but the Yankees lost, four games to three. After the World Series defeat, the Yankees fired manager Casey Stengel.

Maris won the Rawlings Gold Glove Award for fielding excellence. This award honors the top fielders at each position in each league; 18 awards are presented each year. From 1958 to 1964, fellow players voted on the recipients. Maris was also named the American League's Most Valuable Player, beating out Mantle by a vote of 225-222 (the second-closest MVP vote ever). In addition, Maris won the Sultan of Swat Award with a slugging average of .581, along with his 112 RBIs and 39 home runs.

Because of Maris's incredible year in 1960, advertising companies wanted him to endorse their products and appear in television commercials. Roger's brother, Rudy Jr., who had gone into business after polio halted a professional athletic career, came to Maris's aid. Rudy helped Roger sift through the offers and find the worthy ones. Maris did commercials for razor blades and shaving cream and Camel cigarettes. These endorsements brought Maris more money to support his growing family.

At the end of the 1960 season, Maris returned home to Kansas City. He and Pat spent much-needed time together with Susan, Roger Jr., and Kevin. Maris greatly preferred the serenity of his family life to the hounding media following his every move. At home, he could unwind by listening to his

Roger Maris crossed home plate after hitting his thirty-sixth home run of the 1960 season, on September 8 against the Chicago White Sox. Yankee Héctor López *(right)* was next to bat, and he also smashed a home run. Maris finished the season with 39 home runs, and he was named the American League Most Valuable Player.

favorite jazz records or enjoying the outdoors. Maris took solace in Kansas City while he could, though the 1961 season was fast approaching. Maris's most written-about year in baseball was about to begin.

THE M&M BOYS

The country was full of hope and promise at the start of 1961. On January 20, John F. Kennedy was sworn in as the thirty-fifth president of the United States. Like Maris, Kennedy felt a strong obligation to be an active citizen and believed that all Americans shared that duty. In his inauguration speech, the president said to the American people, "Ask not what your country can do for you, ask what you can do for your country."

The 1961 season began with a new Yankee manager. Ralph Houk would try to lead the team to a World Series champion-ship. The season started out roughly for Maris. He was in a slump. In a game against Washington on May 17, Maris hit his fourth home run. Mantle had already hit 10. Maris's batting average was down to .210.

Dan Topping, the president and co-owner of the Yankees, and Roy Hamey, the general manager, spoke to Maris privately. They advised him to stop thinking about averages and go out and play the game. Maris responded. From May 19 to 31, Maris hit 8 home runs, bringing his total for the season to 12. After a short home-run slump in mid-May, Mantle brought his own total for the season to 14 by the end of the month. It seemed that whenever one slugger added a home run to his season total, the other one was sure to follow. Each of them used the pressure of the other's added home run to keep himself on top of his game.

About this time, Mickey Mantle joined Maris and Bob Cerv as a third roommate in the Queens apartment. The three ball-players were good friends, and they all needed a place in which to escape the press. Queens was good for that. The friends were able to go to neighborhood restaurants and walk around outside without hassle, because the press did not spend much time in Queens. Big Julie Isaacson also visited the apartment; the four men played cards, listened to music, and talked. It was an ideal place in which to unwind and get away from it all.

Maris continued the home runs in June. In an early series against Chicago, Maris hit a home run in each of the three games, bringing his home-run count to 15. The day after Maris's fifteenth home run, Mantle got his fifteenth. By June 15, Mantle had 19 home runs and Maris had 22. By June 30,

Roger Maris *(left)* and Mickey Mantle traded the lead in the 1961 home-run race, and soon it became apparent that both players had the chance to break Babe Ruth's season record of 60 home runs, set in 1927. Here, Maris and Mantle looked over a telegram from fans encouraging them in their battle.

Mantle had hit 25 home runs and Maris had hit 27. The press took notice.

By the end of June, it was clear that Roger Maris and Mickey Mantle each had a chance to break the single-season home-run record. Babe Ruth, a former Yankee, had set the record in 1927 with 60 home runs. Many historians believe that the 1927 squad on which Ruth played was the greatest group of ballplayers ever assembled. When Ruth started to hit home run after home run, the fans and the press could not get enough of the slugger. And Ruth loved it. He enjoyed being the center of attention when he played baseball and when he walked down the street.

★ ★ ★ ★ ★ ★

BABE RUTH

George Herman Ruth, Jr., was born on February 6, 1895, in Baltimore, Maryland. He was often alone as a child; his parents left him to take care of himself while they ran a bar. When George was seven years old, his father signed custody of him over to the Catholic brothers who ran St. Mary's Industrial School for Boys. George first learned baseball from Brother Matthias, the prefect of the school.

Jack Dunn of the Baltimore Orioles, then a minor-league team, signed George to the team when George was 19 years old. The players called George "Jack's newest babe" when they saw him. From then on, he was called Babe. That same year, the Boston Red Sox bought his contract, and he made his major-league debut in 1914 as a pitcher. Within a few years, the Red Sox had Ruth play some in the outfield, to take advantage of his hitting abilities.

After the 1919 season, the Red Sox sold Ruth to the New York Yankees. That trade would lead to the storied "Curse of the Bambino." After the trade, the Yankees would go on to win 26 World Series titles, while the Red Sox did not win a World Series until 2004. The Red Sox, it was said, were suffering a curse.

Roger Maris was nothing like Babe Ruth. He was quiet and kept to himself. He did not like to be the center of attention. Home runs were not his idea of helping his team do the best it could—Maris preferred to focus on helping his teammates get into scoring position. But when both Maris and Mantle found themselves knocking out home runs, the press began to call them the M&M Boys. The sale of M&M candies climbed.

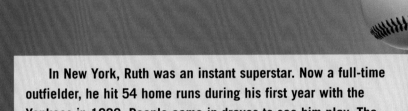

☆ ☆ ☆ ☆ ☆

In New York, Ruth was an instant superstar. Now a full-time outfielder, he hit 54 home runs during his first year with the Yankees in 1920. People came in droves to see him play. The Yankees made so much money that they were able to build a new stadium, which opened in 1923. It was called "The House That Ruth Built." Ruth hit a home run on Opening Day.

Ruth played for the Yankees from 1920 to 1934. In 1921, he hit 59 home runs, and six years later, he broke that record again, with 60 homers. Ruth spent 1935, his last year in the major leagues, as a player and assistant manager with the Boston Braves. He made the switch because he had hoped to become the team's manager the following season, but that did not happen. In one of his last major-league games, Ruth hit three home runs. As Ruth came around the bases the final time, he tipped his cap to the crowd.

Ruth was one of the first five players elected to the Baseball Hall of Fame in 1936. The others were Ty Cobb, Christy Mathewson, Walter Johnson, and Honus Wagner. Even today, Ruth is one of the most honored athletes in the history of the United States.

Newspapers reported each home run in a grid format showing how the M&M Boys compared to Babe Ruth at the same point in the season. Like it or not—the race was on!

154 VS. 162

Both Mantle and Maris were hitting many home runs at the start of July. Their numbers continued to stay close. By the All-Star Game on July 11 (of which both players were a part), Mantle had 29 home runs and Maris had 33. The All-Star Game was played at Candlestick Park in San Francisco, California. The National League team beat the M&M Boys and their American League team, 5-4, in 10 innings. The second All-Star Game was played at Fenway Park in Boston, Massachusetts, later in July, on the 31st. That game would end in a tie after the ninth inning because of a deluge of rain.

During the All-Star break, the media spent a great deal of time writing about the M&M Boys and their chances of breaking Ruth's record. As it became more likely that one of the players could break the record, a debate began. When Ruth had hit 60 home runs in 1927, he played in a 154-game season. Since then, the league had expanded to 10 teams, and the baseball schedule had expanded to a 162-game season. Would it still count if one of the M&M Boys hit 61 *after* 154 games? People across the country debated.

Some people said that it would not be right to count home runs after 154 games, because Ruth might have gotten more home runs himself if he had played a longer season. Fans who had grown up watching Ruth play and felt loyal to their home-run hero did not want to see the record taken away from their idol. Because of this, many of these fans supported the idea that the record had to be broken within 154 games. Ruth's widow, Claire, hoped no one would ever break the record of her husband, who had died in 1948 from throat cancer. Claire told reporters that Babe had wanted to be known as the king of home runs forever.

Other people countered that Ruth might *not* have hit any more home runs—the point being that no one knows and that a season was a season whatever the number of days. Some people also argued that the players in 1961 had more challenges and pressures to face than Ruth did in 1927.

On July 17, baseball commissioner Ford Frick ruled that "a player who hit more than 60 home runs during his club's first 154 games would be recognized as having established a new record." He went on to say that, if a player hit more than 60 home runs after his club's first 154 games, a "distinctive mark" would note in how many games the record was achieved.

THE FANS CHOOSE MANTLE

On July 21, Mantle hit his thirty-seventh home run against Boston; Maris hit his thirty-sixth home run. Then against Chicago on July 25, the Yankees played in a doubleheader. Mantle hit one home run, and Maris hit four; the dueling sluggers were at 40 for Maris and 38 for Mantle. On the following day, something in one of Maris's legs popped as he ran the bases. Because of his leg problem, Maris was not in the starting lineup for the second All-Star Game in Boston. For the rest of July, Maris was in a slump, not able to add to his home-run total at all.

The press started to ask the fans: Whom do you want to win the race? Although Maris had some fans, the majority of the people backed Mantle. Some even wrote letters to the Yankees' manager, Ralph Houk, asking him to change the lineup because they thought Maris had an advantage by hitting right before Mantle. Houk disagreed. He was interested in seeing his club win the pennant. To do that, he believed the lineup order should remain Maris, Mantle, and Yogi Berra.

Like Houk, Maris wanted to lead his team to a pennant. On August 7, Maris hit a bunt that helped his team win the game. Newspaper reporters bombarded Maris. They could not understand why he would choose to jeopardize his home-run race by using up one of his at-bats with a bunt. When he responded honestly that he wanted to help the Yankees to a pennant, they still pressed him. Reporters continued to make Maris feel uneasy, and he did not enjoy talking with them or even being around them. He had a hard time getting reporters to see his point of view accurately. Maris played baseball with the team's success as his top priority. He did not see himself as above bunting, if it meant it would move his team forward. Regardless of how clear this idea seemed to Maris, the press did not understand.

Maris did not hit many home runs between July 26 and August 10, but his success changed in the games that New York played against Washington. During this series, from August 11 to 13, Maris hit his forty-second, forty-third, forty-fourth, and forty-fifth home runs. Then he hit Nos. 46, 47, and 48 on August 15 and 16. At this time, Mantle had 45. Mantle's fans worried about him falling behind Maris.

MEDIA FRENZY

The press and the fans may not have been behind Maris, but his family and friends were. Maris's father called in mid-August to give him encouragement and congratulations. The love and support of his family helped Maris get through his struggling relationship with the press. Amid the excitement and tension of the 1961 season came another special event for Roger and Pat: their fourth child, their third son, Randy, was born. Maris was looking forward to meeting him for the first time while in Kansas City to play the Athletics toward the end of August.

Unfortunately, he could not escape the press. The local newspaper had included his address in the birth announcement for Randy, and reporters lined the streets of his usually quiet neighborhood. Never before had reporters and fans approached Roger and Pat at their home. Now fans knocked on their front door asking for autographs and trying to get a

Mickey Mantle *(left)* congratulated Roger Maris after Maris hit his forty-sixth home run of the 1961 season. Mantle was just off the pace, with 45. Though the press tried to play up a rivalry between the two men, Maris and Mantle were close friends off the field. In fact, they shared an apartment in Queens with teammate Bob Cerv.

peek at the home-run record-chaser. Maris was irate at this invasion of his family's privacy.

From Kansas City, the Yankees traveled to Bloomington, Minnesota, to play three games against the Twins from

August 29 to 31. Many fans from Fargo made the trip to watch Maris, including his father. The Fargo citizens were not let down—they saw some great baseball in that series. Although the Yankees only won one of the three games (they lost the first and the last), and Maris did not add any home runs to his season tally, he played hard, sliding into bases and trying to ensure that his team kept its lead in the pennant race. It was a duel of pitching in the first two games: In game one, Camilo Pascual of the Minnesota Twins kept the Yankees from scoring a single run. On the following night, New York Yankees pitcher Bill Stafford tossed a shutout. Maris had one hit in three at-bats and earned an RBI for the Yankees. The final game of the series was a close one, with the Twins winning 5-4.

Maris had never intended to get caught up in the chase for the single-season home-run record. By the end of August, though, he had hit 51 home runs. He was the first player in history to accomplish this. Mantle was close behind, with 48 home runs. Could the M&M Boys make history in the same number of games as Babe Ruth? People across the country were following the race closely. On August 18, Maris and Mantle appeared on the cover of *Life*. The magazine showed the M&M Boys in front of a picture of Babe Ruth. Inside was a photo essay about the odds of Mantle or Maris breaking the home-run record. Baseball fans had strong feelings regarding the race to break Ruth's record. Some fans still did not want to see it broken. Others wanted to see Mantle break the record. Very few cheered for Maris.

Yankee teammates supported both Maris and Mantle. When pushed by the media to name names, though, most Yankees agreed that it would be nice for Mantle to win, simply because he had been with the team longer, since 1951. None of them felt anything against Maris personally, however. They liked him on and off the field; but the Yankees were rich in tradition and this was only Maris's second season with the team.

Most reporters and sportswriters did not support Maris. They called Maris the Most Vacant Personality (a play on Most Valuable Player). They found Maris sulky or moody and too quiet. Maris did not put on big airs for reporters and try to charm them and be a person he was not. He was serious, and he believed in right and wrong. If he did not think something was right, he did not sit idly and wait to see what would happen. Maris spoke up. He was willing to fight, even when the fight was not popular. Most reporters and sportswriters *did* support Mickey Mantle. They found Mantle charming and quotable. Reporters knew what to expect when they interviewed Mantle. He would not criticize their questions or give a blunt reply.

The two men whom the press had such drastically different views on were, in fact, roommates and close friends. Yet, in addition to the press's insistence on criticizing Maris and placing Mantle on a pedestal, the press also fabricated stories about fights and a brewing rivalry between the two players. Sitting in their apartment together, Mantle would read the newspaper and announce to Maris that they were fighting again. The two friends would laugh. It was difficult on Maris and Mantle, however, to see the press continually fill the newspapers with these inaccuracies and comparisons. The M&M Boys simply wished to be left alone to concentrate on baseball and help their team reach the World Series.

THE STRESS MOUNTS

On September 10, 1961, Maris celebrated his twenty-seventh birthday. Maris did not hit any home runs during the Yankees' doubleheader against the Indians, but the team did win both games and Mantle hit his fifty-third home run. Maris spent the evening with friends Bob Cerv and Big Julie Isaacson at a Manhattan restaurant to celebrate his birthday.

While on the road in Baltimore, Maris stopped at Johns Hopkins Hospital to visit the son of a former baseball player.

The stress and exhaustion that Roger Maris was feeling as he chased Babe Ruth's home-run record is apparent in this picture taken with one game remaining in the 1961 season. By September, Maris had trouble sleeping and some of his hair was falling out.

Maris made sure the press kept his visit out of the papers, because he did not want readers to mistake his purpose for visiting as one for publicity. Since his days in Fargo when he went to the orphanage to toss the football around with the kids, Maris had continued to visit hospitals and give his support and encouragement to children who were suffering. Always, what he asked for in return was for his visits to be kept from the media. During the 1961 season, Maris quietly asked for approval from the Yankees to co-chair the Multiple Sclerosis Society. With their approval, he co-chaired the society with Shirley Temple Black.

Before and after every game, reporters met Maris with the same questions about whether he thought he could beat Ruth's record and how he felt about having to break the record within 154 games. Maris lost sleep, he received hate mail, and he started to lose patches of his hair on the back of his head. Doctors told him the hair loss was stress-related. Maris was not sure he could make it through the season.

On September 15, Maris and the Yankees traveled to Detroit, Michigan, to play a four-game series at Tiger Stadium. The first day was a doubleheader, with single games on the following two days. As had been happening before and after every game, reporters swarmed around Maris. Maris kept his composure and, during the third game, knocked out home run No. 57 of the season.

On the last day in Detroit, he came up to the plate. Something caught his eye in the sky, however, and he stepped out of the batter's box and gazed up. A flock of geese flew over Tiger Stadium. To Maris—during a time in his life when things seemed constantly on the go—this moment of watching the birds soaring through the air was a rarity. He remained out of the batter's box for so long that the umpire took off his outside chest protector to watch the geese, too. When the birds had gone, Maris stepped back into the box, took position, and got ready for the pitch. As gracefully as the birds had been making their way across the sky, Maris sent the ball flying out of the field. Maris had hit home run No. 58.

Maris longed for his family. He longed to be out of the spotlight. Instead, September 20 was rapidly approaching.

And September 20 brought with it something that the media and seemingly the entire city of New York could not ignore: the 154th game of the 1961 season. Going into the September 20 game, Maris had 58 home runs—two away from matching Ruth's record. Mantle had only 53; the nation knew he was out of the race. It was up to Maris. Would Roger Maris beat Babe Ruth's record? The country held its breath.

Records Are Made to Be Broken

The 154th game took place on September 20. The New York Yankees faced the Baltimore Orioles at Memorial Stadium in Maryland. So far, Roger Maris had not hit a home run at this stadium in 1961. Now Maris would need to hit three of them to break Babe Ruth's home-run record in the same number of games as Ruth hit 60. The chances were slim.

Not everyone with an interest in Maris's quest could be at the game in person. Mickey Mantle was out of the lineup that night because of an abscessed hip, which developed after he received an injection for a cold. Pat Maris watched the game from the KMBC-TV studio in Kansas City. Claire Ruth, Babe's widow, watched the game from her apartment in Manhattan. During Maris's first at-bat, he hit a line drive to right field. Earl Robinson caught the ball, and Maris was out. At Maris's next at-bat, he let one ball go. He swung and missed at the second. He let another ball go. On the fourth pitch, Maris swung. The ball left the field for his fifty-ninth home run. He was one away from tying Ruth's record.

In his third at-bat, he struck out. Maris came up to bat a fourth time in the seventh inning, but Robinson once again caught the ball and Maris was out. Maris's fifth and final at-bat came in the ninth inning. The Orioles brought out Hall of Famer Hoyt Wilhelm, a knuckleball pitcher with an ERA of 2.52. Wilhelm's first pitch was a knuckleball, and Maris had his first strike. Wilhelm's second pitch went low, and Maris fouled it off. Maris made contact on the third swing, but he was out at first.

Although Maris had not reached Ruth's 60-home-run mark, he had already had a blockbuster season. The day before the 155th game of the season, Maris received, for the second year straight, the Sultan of Swat Award. Then at the 155th game, the Baltimore Orioles presented Maris with a three-foot trophy as a tribute to his outstanding sportsmanship. The inscription noted "the ultimate respect and admiration of Oriole fans." Maris was touched and thankful.

Roger was thrilled to have Pat join him when the Yankees returned to New York. There were four regular-season games left, and Pat planned to be at Roger's side during that time. The couple spent as much time together as possible, enjoying topics and events other than baseball. Roger had a chance to look at pictures of Susan, Roger Jr., Kevin, and Randy and hear detailed stories about their daily routines and special adventures. The extended time with Pat helped Roger to refocus and reduce his stress.

As the season was nearing its end, Maris, Mantle, and Bob Cerv said good-bye to Big Julie's Queens apartment for the year. Cerv was in the hospital recovering from knee surgery, and Mantle and Maris would each find new living accommodations the following season. For the remainder of the season, the Marises and the Mantles moved into Loew's Midtown Hotel in Manhattan.

61 IN '61

On September 26, 1961, Roger Maris made history. Up against Baltimore pitcher Jack Fisher in the third inning, Maris faced a two-ball, two-strike count. There were two outs. But Maris slammed the high curveball into the upper right-field stands, hitting his sixtieth home run of the year. Roger Maris had tied Babe Ruth's record. The home run came at Maris's 684th plate appearance. (Ruth hit his sixtieth home run at his 689th plate appearance.) Following the strike of the bat and the ball soaring into the stands, Maris made his lap around the bases in his typical style: head lowered, giving a high-five to the third-base coach as he rounded third, and quickly making his way to the dugout after crossing home plate. No flash and no excess.

The crowd of 19,000 at Yankee Stadium rose to its feet and cheered and applauded until Maris's teammates pushed him back out of the dugout to wave his cap and let the fans get another look at him. Maris modestly complied. Pat was beside herself with happiness for her husband. Rudy Sr. was thrilled for his son. Roger's mother, Anne Corrine, got tears in her eyes, as she had with every home run he had hit that season.

In the next two games, Maris did not hit any home runs. Doctors admitted Mantle to the hospital for a hip infection on September 29. He would miss the last few days of the season. He cheered Maris on from his hospital bed. Maris's last chance to pass Ruth's record came on the last day of the season, October 1.

Maris began his day as he did most other game days—with a baloney-and-egg breakfast at a New York deli. (Maris was quite particular about his eggs and only liked the way certain people made them. When he ate at the apartment with Cerv and Mantle, he would not eat the eggs they cooked. There he

Roger Maris watched his record-breaking sixty-first home run leave Yankee Stadium on the last day of the season, October 1, 1961. It was the only run of the day, as the Yankees beat the Red Sox, 1-0.

only ate eggs that he had made.) On this day, the New York Yankees would play the Boston Red Sox.

Game time arrived, and Maris came up to bat. Tracy Stallard was pitching for the Red Sox. Maris went hitless at his first at-bat. From the stands, 23,154 fans watched Maris step up to the plate a second time in the fourth inning. The score was 0-0. The season had taken a lot out of Maris—he was tired, stressed out, and physically worn down. Each home run that brought him closer to breaking Ruth's record had left him drained and mentally exhausted.

As Maris took his position, the crowd hushed. Could he do it? The fans rose to their feet in anticipation. The first pitch was a ball, outside. The fans began to boo. The second pitch was a ball, low. The fans booed again. The third pitch was a fastball, and Maris connected. The announcer shouted excitedly, "Fastball, hit deep to right! This could be it! Way back there! Holy cow, he did it! Sixty-one for Maris!"

Reaching the sixth row of the lower deck in right field, Maris's home run had broken Ruth's record. Maris had managed the only run scored—the Yankees beat the Red Sox 1-0. Maris rounded the bases just as he had on his first home run and just as he had on his sixtieth home run—with no extra show. As he rounded third, he shook hands with the third-base coach, Frank Crosetti. A giddy fan jumped onto the field and shook hands with Maris as he trotted past. After crossing home plate, he tried to make his way to the dugout, but the players would not let him in. Embarrassed, Maris stepped back onto the field to wave his cap to the crowd. The fans gave him a rousing standing ovation.

The home-run ball flew into the right-field seats, and a 21-year-old truck driver named Sal Durante caught the ball. Sam Gordon, who owned a restaurant, offered Durante $5,000 for the ball. Gordon planned to display the ball in his restaurant. Durante first asked Maris if he wanted the ball back, but Maris would not accept it. Maris had heard that the young man planned to get married, and he thought Durante could use the money to get started. Gordon displayed the ball in his restaurant until he eventually gave it back to Maris. Maris promptly gave it to the Hall of Fame, along with the bat he used.

THE AFTERMATH

The publicity and commotion that followed Maris breaking Ruth's record was intense. Maris later told an interviewer,

Spectators at Yankee Stadium try to catch Roger Maris's sixty-first home-run ball in the right-field stands. The ball was caught by Sal Durante, who asked Maris if he wanted it back. A restaurateur offerred Durante $5,000 for the ball, and since Maris heard that the young man was about to get married, he let Durante keep the ball so he could start his marriage having money.

"Sometimes I wish I never hit those 61 home runs. All I want is to be treated like any other player. I never wanted all this hoopla. All I wanted was to be a good ballplayer, hit 25 or 30 homers, drive in around a hundred runs, hit .280, and help my club win pennants. I just wanted to be one of the guys, an average player with a good season." Maris had proved himself anything but average.

Ford Frick, commissioner of baseball, stood by his decision to list Maris's record with a qualifying note saying that Maris had played a 162-game schedule. The *Book of Baseball Records* (then called *The Little Red Book*) read, "Most Home Runs, season, 61-Roger E. Maris, A.L., N.Y., 1961 (162-game season); 60-George H. Ruth, A.L., N.Y., 1927 (154-game season)." *Sporting News Record Book* listed the home-run record in a similar fashion. No other record broken after the season was extended was noted this way in the record books. Frick's decision held for 30 years, until 1991, when baseball commissioner Fay Vincent declared Maris the sole and official record holder.

President John F. Kennedy wrote a letter to Maris after he broke the record. It read: "The American people will always admire a man who overcomes great pressures to achieve an outstanding goal." Maris was moved by the president's sentiments.

The season was not over quite yet. As the winners of the American League pennant, the New York Yankees earned a spot in the 1961 World Series against the Cincinnati Reds. Maris had only 2 hits in his 19 at-bats over the course of the five games, but his hits were helpful to the winning outcome: He had one double and one home run; he scored four runs and hit two RBIs. The Yankees won four of the five games played, earning themselves the World Series title.

The American League named Maris the Most Valuable Player for a second straight year. Not many baseball players have ever accomplished this feat. Maris is in a category with greats like Mickey Mantle, Yogi Berra, Jimmie Foxx, Ernie Banks, and Joe Morgan. Maris had led the American League with 142 runs batted in and 366 total bases. Maris tied Mantle for most runs in the American League with 132.

He won other awards as well. He won the Sultan of Swat Award, the Associated Press Professional Athlete of the Year, the B'nai B'rith Award, *Sports Illustrated* Sportsman of the Year, the *Sporting News* Player of the Year, the Catholic Athlete of the Year, and the Hickok Belt as the best professional athlete of the year. The Hickok Belt was established in 1950 by the Hickok Manufacturing Company, which produced men's

☆ ☆ ☆ ☆ ☆

1961 HOME-RUN RACE

The following chart shows on what date Mickey Mantle and Roger Maris hit each of their home runs during the 1961 race to beat Babe Ruth's record. The lead in the home-run race yo-yoed between Maris and Mantle. The New York media took great interest in the race and printed daily articles, keeping careful track of the M&M Boys. After September 5, Mantle started to slow down, but Maris kept his momentum going. Maris broke Ruth's record on the last day of the season, October 1, 1961.

Date	Mantle	Maris	Date	Mantle	Maris
April 17	1		May 30	12, 13	10, 11
April 20	2, 3		May 31	14	12
April 21	4		June 2		13
April 23	5		June 3		14
April 26	6, 7	1	June 4		15
May 2	8		June 5	15	
May 3		2	June 6		16
May 4	9		June 7		17
May 6		3	June 9	16	18
May 16	10		June 10	17	
May 17		4	June 11	18	19, 20
May 19		5	June 13		21
May 20		6	June 14		22
May 21		7	June 15	19	
May 24		8	June 17	20	23
May 28		9	June 18		24
May 29	11		June 19		25

high-end accessories, in memory of the company's founder. The belt was presented to the top athlete of the year (in 1960 Arnold Palmer won the belt for his achievements in golf, and

☆ ☆ ☆ ☆ ☆

Date	Mantle	Maris	Date	Mantle	Maris
June 20		26	August 6	41, 42, 43	
June 21	21, 22		August 11	44	42
June 22		27	August 12		43
June 26	23		August 13	45	44, 45
June 28	24		August 15		46
June 30	25		August 16		47, 48
July 1	26, 27	28	August 20	46	49
July 2	28	29, 30	August 22		50
July 4		31	August 26		51
July 5		32	August 30	47	
July 8	29		August 31	48	
July 9		33	September 2		52, 53
July 13	30	34	September 3	49, 50	
July 14	31		September 5	51	
July 15		35	September 6		54
July 16	32		September 7		55
July 17	33		September 8	52	
July 18	34, 35		September 9		56
July 19	36		September 10	53	
July 21	37	36	September 16		57
July 25	38	37, 38, 39, 40	September 17		58
			September 20		59
July 26	39		September 23	54	
August 2	40		September 26		60
August 4		41	October 1		61

In the off-season after his record-breaking year, Roger Maris had the opportunity to appear on the big screen and the small screen. One movie he filmed was *That Touch of Mink*, with Doris Day and Cary Grant. Here during a break in shooting were *(from left)* Mickey Mantle, Day, Grant, Maris, and Yogi Berra.

in 1959, Ingemar Johansson had won for boxing). The trophy was an alligator-skin belt with a solid gold buckle, a 4-carat diamond, and 26 gem chips. The Hickok Company presented Maris with the belt at the Rochester Press-Radio Club's annual children's charity dinner.

Like the Hickok Belt, nearly all of the awards that Maris won had presentation ceremonies, banquets, or both, which

Maris attended. The quiet, non-celebratory celebrity found himself often feeling awkward and out of place. He did not feel comfortable dressed up and doted upon. The press continued to ask such repetitive questions that Maris took to using stock responses. As a result, the press portrayed him to the public as boring, uninterested in baseball, and undeserving of passing Ruth's record.

ROGER IN THE MOVIES

Besides the award ceremonies, Maris took on other projects during the off-season. He appeared on *The Perry Como Show*, a popular TV variety show. He allowed his name (as did Mantle) to be used on a line of men's and boys' clothing. The lucrative deal would guarantee Maris and Mantle $45,000 a year each for three years. Maris endorsed some food and household products by appearing in television and print advertisements. Another opportunity that Maris agreed to was the writing of his story. Maris chose friend and sportswriter Jim Ogle to co-author his book, *Roger Maris at Bat*. The book was not widely read, reviewed, or printed. Today it remains hard to find.

Movie producers offered Maris a number of acting parts in films as a result of the widespread media coverage in 1961. Because the roles in the movies were small, he was able to do them during the off-season without taking much time away from what mattered to him the most.

In April 1962, *Safe at Home!* opened in New York theaters. The movie is about a little boy who tells his Little League friends that his father knows Mickey Mantle and Roger Maris and the trouble that his lie causes. The movie did not receive good reviews. Maris also had a small part in a romantic comedy starring Cary Grant and Doris Day called *That Touch of Mink*. Grant's and Day's characters come to a Yankee game in the film, and Maris, Mantle, and Yogi Berra appear in the film as themselves. The movie opened in theaters in June 1962. *That Touch of Mink* did receive good reviews from critics; it was nominated for three Oscars and won a Golden Globe for best comedy.

Many years later, in the fall of 1980, Maris appeared in a short scene as himself in another movie, called *It's My Turn.* The romantic comedy is about a math professor who falls in love with the son of her father's bride; the son is a former Yankee player who retired prematurely. Critics gave the movie poor reviews.

During the off-season, Maris could have taken on many more projects and earned a great deal more money, but more often than not, he turned down public appearances and other offers. He did not even think twice—Maris's family came first.

Last Years
with the Yankees

Now that Roger Maris had broken Babe Ruth's record, the world wanted to know if he would do it again. Would he go for 62 in '62? Maris had had quite enough of the prodding press, the repetitive questions, and the endless stress. He was ready for life to get back to normal.

During the off-season, Maris returned home to Pat and his four children, Susan, Roger Jr., Kevin, and Randy. The family took part in community and church events, entertained with close friends, and did their best to stay out of the spotlight. Maris at last had time to relax thoroughly, through golfing, bowling, and hunting. He did wood-working projects around the house, including making a cedar chest. Comedian Bob Hope invited the couple to watch the Rose Bowl Parade from his private box. Roger and Pat traveled to Pasadena, California, to see the famous parade, which features floats made entirely of flowers.

BACK TO THE GAME

One bit of business that Maris needed to take care of before the new season opened was negotiating his salary. In 1961, he had made $42,000; Mickey Mantle had made $75,000. After multiple meetings, Maris and the Yankees agreed on a figure: In 1962, Maris would earn $72,500 with an additional $5,000 for living expenses. His salary made him the fourth-highest-paid New York Yankee in history. To date, the highest-paid players had been Joe DiMaggio ($100,000), Mickey Mantle ($82,000 that year), and Babe Ruth ($80,000).

Maris also took on a new roommate for the 1962 season. He shared Big Julie Isaacson's Queens apartment with a former Pittsburgh Pirates ballplayer named Dale Long. As Maris had experienced the previous year, he found an oasis in the apartment. He was often able to enjoy some privacy and solitude there during another stressful season.

Maris had not established a good relationship with the press during 1961. It was no surprise, therefore, when the press portrayed Maris unfavorably to the public during the off-season; in fact, reporters made him out to be anti-baseball. According to press coverage, Maris was a fluke—someone who took away Ruth's record by chance instead of skill. Reporters filled newspapers with articles about how Maris had taken advantage of Yankee Stadium's short right-field porch, referring to the fact that right field in the stadium is shorter than in most other ballparks. Some people thought these home runs were somehow less worthy and "cheap." Yet in fact, Maris hit only 30 of his 61 home runs in Yankee Stadium. He hit the other 31 home runs on the road. Now, faced with a new season, neither the press nor the fans were behind Maris.

Still, the season got off to a good start. On Opening Day—April 10—Maris hit his first home run with two men on base,

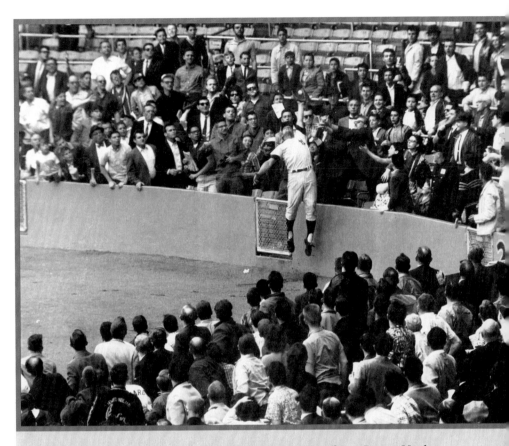

Leaping high above the outfield wall at Yankee Stadium, Roger Maris saved a ball hit by Washington Senator Ken Retzer from going into the stands for a home run in May 1962. Despite spectacular plays like this one, the fans and the media often criticized Maris for the season he was having in 1962.

in a game against the Baltimore Orioles. The second game of the season took the Yankees on the road to Detroit to play against the Tigers. There, Maris had a close call when a jeering fan threw a soda bottle at him while he was in right field. The bottle broke next to Maris, and a piece of broken glass nearly cut him on the arm.

By mid-May, Maris had hit six home runs and gotten his batting average up to .309, but then injury struck. On May 16, the Yankees were at Fenway Park to play the Boston Red Sox. Working right field, Maris made a flying leap to try to stop Carl Yastrzemski's ball from going over the fence for a home run. Maris could not reach it; instead, he strained a groin muscle and was out until May 22.

Fans frequently booed the once-hot home-run slugger. He tried to put the jeering fans and critical reporters out of his mind. In June, Maris hit .202 and had only seven home runs. Then for the remainder of the season, he gradually brought his numbers up. He was again voted to the All-Star Game, which took place on July 10 at D.C. Stadium in Washington, D.C., with a second game on July 30 at Wrigley Field in Chicago. The American League lost the game in Washington but won in Chicago.

Maris continued to raise his batting average throughout July, batting .256 that month, with an impressive .554 slugging average and 24 RBIs. Nonetheless, angry fans hit him with golf balls and a beer can during a game. They yelled obscenities at him. In August, his batting average was .264.

By the end of the 1962 season, Maris had hit 33 home runs and 34 doubles, and scored 92 runs. He drove in 100 RBIs with a batting average of .256. Maris played in both All-Star Games—his fourth straight year participating. Maris's teammate, Mickey Mantle, won the Most Valuable Player award that year—batting .321 with 30 home runs.

The New York Yankees again made it to the World Series—their third straight. In the 1962 Series, the Yankees were up against the San Francisco Giants. Maris and Mantle had less than impressive batting numbers; Maris hit just .174, while Mantle was even worse at .120. Maris was able to hit one home run; Mantle none. Although Maris had only 4 hits in his 23 at-bats during the seven-game series, he had 5 RBIs—more than anyone else on the Yankee roster. Maris made an impressive showing in the field, as well. When Maris managed to cut off a hit from Willie Mays and return the ball to the infield quickly from an off-balance stance, he saved the Yankees from losing their 1-0 lead in the ninth inning of the decisive Game 7. The Yankees won the Series, four games to three.

INJURIES TAKE THEIR TOLL

During the off-season, Maris returned home to be with Pat and Susan, Roger Jr., Kevin, and Randy. He quickly settled into backyard barbecues and welcomed the opportunity to tinker with projects around the house. "Home" was now in Independence, Missouri.

Maris did not go through another salary negotiation before the start of the 1963 season. He avoided the hassle that a negotiation brought by agreeing to a salary freeze at the 1962 level. Maris hoped that the fans and the press would ease up now that a year separated him from his '61 feat. He was simply eager to play baseball and not to feel the public's constant pressure and criticism.

Yet, during spring training and the exhibition games, Maris struggled with injuries. In April, he tore his left hamstring muscle, which caused him to miss the first seven games of the season. Later in the month, he injured the same muscle and had to miss another three games. Then in May, he pulled a back muscle and had to miss three games. The injuries continued in June, when he experienced a contusion of the left big toe, but he played through the injury.

Despite his toe injury and his earlier time away from the game, Maris produced good numbers during June, and by early July, he was batting at .300. Using his impressive offense (solid hitting and aggressive base running) and dependable defense (catching deep hits at the wall and throwing balls back to the infield with speed and precision), Maris helped the Yankees win ball games.

His stays on the disabled list continued in July, however, when Maris underwent surgery and had to miss 17 games. For the first time in four years, Maris was not voted to the All-Star team. Following the break, his list of ailments continued: a bruised heel, a muscle spasm, a strained hand, a strained back, and a sore lower back.

☆ ☆ ☆ ☆ ☆ ☆

MARIS'S NUMBER-ONE FAN

Roger Maris had many fans in New York, including one boy named Andy Strasberg who grew up watching and admiring Maris. When Andy entered Yankee Stadium, he usually bought a general-admission ticket, but a police officer who monitored the stands let him switch to an empty reserved seat. The one that Andy came to sit in most was in Section 31, Row 162-A, Seat 1. It overlooked right field, where he could watch his hero: Roger Maris.

Andy liked to come two hours early to the games so that he could watch Maris park his car and walk to the stadium. Andy shyly introduced himself and started to say hello when Maris passed. Andy came to so many Yankee games that Maris began to recognize him. Once, Andy worked up the courage to ask Maris for a bat that he had used to hit a home run. Maris told Andy that he would give him the next bat he used to hit a homer. Just days after their conversation, Maris hit a home run during a game on the road. Andy was not sure if Maris would remember his request. Maris, though, saw his promise through. The first game back at Yankee Stadium, Maris had a stadium worker track down Andy and give him the home-run bat.

Andy grew up to become a marketer for the San Diego Padres. After working with the club for 22 years, he created ACME (All-Star Corporate Marketing Enterprises). He became, and remains, a close friend of the Maris family. In 1990, Roger's son Randy and his wife, Fran, called Andy to ask him to be the godfather of their newborn baby, Andrew.

In all, Maris played in only 90 games during the 1963 season under manager Ralph Houk. Despite missing almost a half-season's worth of games, Maris still hit 23 home runs and drove in 53 RBIs. The Yankees played in the World Series for the fourth year straight, this time against the Los Angeles Dodgers. The Dodgers boasted a left-handed pitcher named Sandy Koufax, who had struck out 306 batters during the season. He started Game 1 against the Yankees and struck out the first five batters: Tony Kubek, Bobby Richardson, Tom Tresh, Mickey Mantle, and Roger Maris. The Dodgers went on to sweep the Series in four games; the Yankees could not manage a single win. After the season, Ralph Houk moved to the Yankees' front office as the team's general manager.

PLAYING FOR YOGI BERRA

After making it through the endless injuries of 1963, Maris was relieved to return to family life. Tragedy struck the nation, however, when President John F. Kennedy was shot on November 21, 1963. The president had been in Texas to give political speeches. He was riding in an open car past crowds of cheering onlookers in Dallas when he was shot. Soon after, the president died. Across the country, people felt tremendous sadness over this loss.

In January 1964, the governor of North Dakota acknowledged Maris when he presented the ballplayer with the Theodore Roosevelt Rough Rider Award. The award, established in 1961, is given to prominent North Dakotans. Previous winners included entertainer Lawrence Welk, actress Dorothy Stickney, and artist Ivan Dmitri.

By the beginning of spring training in February, a little more than two months after the Kennedy assassination, the nation had begun to heal and was looking ahead to happier days. Maris, too, needed to focus on what the future held. He took a pay cut entering the 1964 season but felt it was justified after having played only 90 games the season before. He

During spring training in 1964, Roger Maris and Mickey Mantle got together with the Yankees' new manager, Yogi Berra. Maris was hoping to rebound from the previous season, when a string of injuries kept him off the field for nearly half the games.

was looking forward to the '64 season with the new Yankees manager, Yogi Berra. Maris had played and become friends with Berra in 1961. Berra and Maris got along well, and Maris felt that he might have the chance to enjoy the game of baseball once again this season.

Unfortunately, the New York Yankees were an aging team, and soon, the team found itself in third place; Baltimore and Chicago led the American League. By the start of September, Berra realized that Mickey Mantle could no longer cover center field, so he moved Maris from right field to center field and

Mantle to right field. Following the move, the Yankees were able to climb in front of Chicago, into second place.

With solid hitting in early September, Maris helped the team regain first place on September 17. Maris finished the season with 26 home runs and 71 RBIs. His batting average of .281 nearly matched what he had done in 1960.

The numbers Maris produced greatly contributed to the overall success of the Yankees, giving them the opportunity to play in the 1964 World Series against the St. Louis Cardinals. In the seven-game series, Maris hit one home run and had a batting average of .200. The Yankees lost the Series, four games to three. The Yankees fired Berra as manager.

A BROKEN HAND AND A BROKEN SPIRIT

With Maris's success in the 1964 season, the Yankees offered him a return to the salary he had received in 1962 and 1963. Maris appreciated going back to the higher salary. At home, Maris kept busy with his large family—he now had five children: Susan, Roger Jr., Kevin, Randy, and baby Richard. Pat and the children treasured their time with Roger. At heart, Maris was a true family man and took pride in each of his children's successes. Roger Jr., about seven years old, and Kevin, about six years old, started to take their first interest in baseball. They practiced throws and catching with a baseball mitt, and they tried out swinging a bat. Roger and Pat kept a careful eye on their children's grades and helped them strive for academic success.

Johnny Keane came in as manager of the New York Yankees in 1965. Although the 1964 season had worked out very well for Maris, it looked as if 1965 was going to be a repeat of 1963. In late April, Maris was put on the disabled list for 26 games when he pulled a thigh muscle making an impressive backhanded catch of Bert Campaneris's line drive to right-center field. Not long after returning from that injury, Maris slammed his pinky and ring fingers into umpire Bill Haller's shoe when he slid across home plate on June 20. Maris missed another five games.

Eight days after his slide into the umpire, Maris still could not properly grip a baseball bat. Nonetheless, he was in the lineup. On one pitch, Maris heard a pop in his right hand as he tried to swing at the ball; his hand immediately started to swell. Maris struck out. The Yankees ordered X-rays of his hand, but they did not talk to Maris about their findings. They continued to put him in the lineup, despite his insistence that he was in pain. The media started to portray Maris as a slough-off, someone who had stopped caring about the game and did not really want to play. They made him out to be a whiner and assumed he was faking his insistence on pain.

Finally, Big Julie Isaacson, Maris's good friend who had helped him make his way in New York when he first arrived, told Maris that he would help him. He took Maris to the best

★ ★ ★ ★ ☆

HUMBLE AT HEART

Although the New York press made Roger Maris out to be flippant, moody, and sullen, his friends and family remember him as a caring, humble man. Maris tried to return to Missouri whenever he could to be with his family. One day, he took a plane back to Kansas City immediately after a game. He and his family went out for coffee to spend a bit of time together before he had to fly back to New York. Maris said nothing about the Yankees game he had just played; he just listened to news from home. But after two patrons approached Maris to compliment him on his game, Maris admitted to his family that he had hit two home runs and seven RBIs.

In a game on June 20, 1965, against the Minnesota Twins, Roger Maris was injured sliding into home plate when his right hand slammed into the umpire. The Yankees kept Maris in the lineup despite his insistence that he was in pain. Eventually, Maris learned that he had broken a bone in the hand.

doctor he could find, without the knowledge of the Yankee management. After X-rays and exams, Maris and Isaacson listened to the doctor's diagnosis. Maris had a broken bone in his hand. In addition, a fragment of the bone had lodged itself into the upper right side of his hand. Maris was stunned. He went to talk to the Yankee management but was even more surprised to find out that some people within the organization had known the severity of his condition and had not said anything. They had kept it from Maris, from the other Yankee players, from the press, and from the fans.

Maris's doctor told him he would need surgery. Maris was not sure an operation was necessary, but when he heard that he would eventually lose all ability to move those fingers, he agreed to the procedure. Dr. J. William Littler performed the surgery to remove the fragment on September 28 at Roosevelt Hospital. Although Maris did not openly criticize the team's management for its lack of action, relations between Maris and the New York Yankees would never be the same.

HANGING UP HIS PINSTRIPES

Due to the severity of the ailments Maris faced in 1965, he played in only 46 games—with only 155 at-bats. He hit 8 home runs and 27 RBIs, and finished with a .239 batting average. In addition, Maris did lose some strength in two fingers on his right hand, even with the corrective surgery.

Maris left the '65 season feeling low. He wanted to be playing baseball—not spending his time in doctor's offices and hospitals. With the surgery and recovery time behind him, Maris spent his off-season hunting, playing golf, and—just as the 1966 season began—enjoying the thrill that came with the birth of his second daughter, Sandra, his and Pat's sixth child.

Maris felt good going into spring training, but both he and the New York Yankees had a slow start to the season. The Yankees, in fact, were playing so poorly that management fired Johnny Keane and brought Ralph Houk back as manager. Maris played better after the change in managers. Then in May, in a game against the Tigers, Maris got caught under catcher Bill Freehan's shin guard while trying to slide home. As a result, Maris sprained his knee. For the rest of the season, the knee caused him problems.

Later in May, the Yankees were up against the California Angels. Maris caught a ball in right field that Jim Piersall had fired toward the back wall. As Maris snagged the ball, he slammed hard into the wall and crumpled to the ground. Paramedics carried Maris off the field on a stretcher. Luckily, the injury was not serious, aside from substantial bruising.

On Friday, September 30, 1966, Maris and the New York Yankees played against the Chicago White Sox at Comiskey Park. This would be Maris's last time in the Yankees' famous pinstripe uniform. As had happened so many times since 1961, fans booed Maris when he came to the plate. This was his one and only time at the plate during the game; he was being used as a pinch hitter. In his final Yankee at-bat, in which he was jeered by the Chicago fans, Roger Maris took his last swing: a home run that earned him two RBIs.

After the 1966 season ended, Maris had plans to retire. He talked to Houk about this, but Houk encouraged Maris to wait to make any decisions until spring training. Perhaps, with the off-season to think over his future, Maris would change his mind. Maris agreed. Rumors started up in the press that Maris might move back to Fargo and that he had been looking for business opportunities.

When Yankee general manager Lee MacPhail heard of these rumors, he called Maris to talk about his plans. Maris told MacPhail about his conversation with Houk. Then Maris asked if MacPhail had any plans to trade him, because if he did, Maris would announce his retirement now instead of waiting for spring training. MacPhail assured Maris that he had no trade plans.

Days after this conversation, on December 8, 1966, the Yankees traded Roger Maris to the St. Louis Cardinals of the National League. Maris had known nothing about the deal. The shock of the trade came not only to Maris but also to the baseball community. The Yankees traded Maris for Charley Smith, an average ballplayer with average stats.

Maris was not happy with the New York Yankees. Although Maris had planned to leave baseball altogether, he did not want to give the press the opportunity to put a false twist on the story by announcing that Maris had quit because he had been traded from the Yankees. Plus, Maris did not want to let the Cardinals down. St. Louis was only a 45-minute plane ride from Independence, so playing on the Cardinals would give Maris more time with his family and friends. He signed a $75,000 contract with the Cardinals.

7

A Fresh
Start

Management for the St. Louis Cardinals looked forward to adding Roger Maris to the team's lineup. In 1966, the Cards had come in sixth place in the National League, and they thought that Maris's determination and drive to win would benefit their team. The players, however, were not sure what to think about Maris coming to the team.

Everyone soon found out what kind of player—and person—Maris was. The Cardinals played the New York Mets in an exhibition game before the start of the regular season. Maris provided four hits for the team. He also gave the Cardinals a taste of his aggressive base running when he made it home from third base off a short fly ball to left field. In the opening game against the San Francisco Giants on April 11, 1967, Maris turned a single into a double with his speed on the bases. The crowd cheered in appreciation.

The Cardinals played a game against the Pittsburgh Pirates at Forbes Field on May 9. Andy Strasberg, who had been a Roger Maris fan since he was a child, was in the stands and caught Maris's home-run ball. The home run was Maris's first as a player in the National League. It was a day of number "9" coincidences: the date was May 9; Maris wore uniform No. 9; the ball fell into Seat 9 of Row 9.

LIFE IN ST. LOUIS

Maris was relaxed, happy, healthy, close to home, and enjoying life. He soon made good friends with some of his Cardinal teammates, in particular Mike Shannon. Shannon played his entire nine-year career with the Cardinals, from 1962 to 1970. Maris and Shannon enjoyed fun times together. Their wives and children also got along, and the two families shared the season's highs and lows.

The move from New York to St. Louis allowed Maris to fall in love with baseball all over again. At home games, he could often look into the crowd to see his children and Pat watching, something that brought him much delight. Maris himself was one of the Cardinals' biggest fans. On days he was out of the lineup, he sat in the dugout and shouted words of encouragement to his teammates. In clutch situations, Maris had more RBIs than anyone on the team.

Due, in part, to Maris's contributions to the club, the St. Louis Cardinals were heading to the World Series. In the '67 Series against the Boston Red Sox, Maris hit a home run and set a Cardinal record with seven RBIs. His batting average soared to .385. Maris played every inning of the seven-game series, even though he was sick with a fever and had shoulder pain throughout. After the seventh game, Maris's doctor gave him a shot of Novocain and cortisone to relieve the pain in his

Now with the St. Louis Cardinals, Roger Maris took a swing during the 1967 World Series against the Boston Red Sox. He set a Cardinal record with seven RBIs during the Series. Maris also set a record for appearing in more World Series games in the 1960s than any other player.

shoulder. The St. Louis Cardinals won the World Series, four games to three.

THE LAST DAYS WITH THE CARDINALS

Maris signed a second $75,000 contract with the Cardinals for the 1968 season. He also made a deal with August Busch, the owner of the Cardinals, for a beer distributorship covering eight counties near Gainesville, Florida. Roger and his brother, Rudy, would run the distributorship together.

During this time, Maris disclosed that he had Bell's palsy, which causes temporary weakening or paralysis of facial muscles because of trauma to the seventh cranial nerve. The condition affects about 40,000 Americans every year. The Bell's palsy affected Maris's right cheek, and its paralysis made it impossible for him to blink his right eye. The inability to blink made his vision blurry. Luckily, the condition usually lasts only a short time, from a few days to a few weeks. Doctors announced that Maris was improved by January.

For the remainder of the off-season, Maris relaxed in Independence with his family. He also accepted the Bob Bauman Physical Comeback Award from the St. Louis Chapter of the Baseball Writers' Association of America. The award made Maris feel good about his determination to fight through his numerous illnesses and ailments and keep returning to baseball.

After spring training, the Cardinals went on to enjoy another winning season in 1968. Maris's base-running skills still impressed fans and players alike. In one game against the New York Mets on June 2—the second game of a double-header—Maris made an extraordinary play. It was the seventh inning. The score was tied, 2-2. Maris came up to bat and hit a single. Orlando Cepeda was up next. He hit a pop-fly single. Maris ran the bases so quickly, however, he was able to score off the single and win the game for the Cardinals.

As Maris went through the 1968 season, he found that his body was unable to keep up the way it had in the past. He was often sitting on the bench, used as a pinch hitter instead of in the starting lineup. Maris decided not to wait until the end of the season: On August 5, he announced that he would retire from baseball at the end of the season. He hit his last regular-season home run off Don Wilson on September 15. It was home run No. 275.

On September 29, the Cardinals honored Maris for his baseball achievements before the game began. His family was at the ceremony: Pat, Susan, Roger Jr., Kevin, Randy, Richard, and Sandra. Big Julie Isaacson came from New York to be part of the ceremony, as did Andy Strasberg, whom Maris called his "number-one fan." The St. Louis Cardinals and the fans thought much of Maris—his knowledge about baseball, his skill as a batter and in the field, and his warm and humble demeanor. Maris was a first-class act in every regard, and St. Louis took the opportunity to show him its appreciation.

The '68 World Series, in which the Cardinals lost to the Detroit Tigers, four games to three, brought little enjoyment to the Cardinals or to Maris. The Cardinals started with a three-games-to-one lead, but the Tigers fought back to win three straight and capture the Series. Maris's 16-year baseball career was over. He had played in seven World Series: more World Series games in the 1960s than any other player in baseball.

FROM BASEBALL TO BEER

Roger, Pat, and the children relocated after Maris retired from baseball. The family moved to Gainesville, Florida. There, they could move into the next chapter of their lives: running the beer distributorship. Roger's brother, Rudy, took care of the management aspects, while Roger handled the public side of the business.

Maris took a hands-on approach to his work, driving delivery trucks and talking to pub owners personally. Business boomed. When the workers went on strike to see how the Maris brothers would respond to their demands, the entire Maris family pitched in to save the distributorship from going under. They loaded and drove delivery trucks. The workers ended the strike, and the business continued to prosper.

Maris was settling into his new life after baseball. The world was a much different place than it had been in the 1940s, growing up in North Dakota. Space exploration had reached new heights. Americans landed a man on the moon on

July 20, 1969. On this historic day, astronauts Neil Armstrong and Edwin Aldrin Jr. landed the *Eagle* lunar module on the moon. Armstrong took the first step on the moon shortly after, and he and Aldrin positioned the American flag on the moon's surface.

The Vietnam War, which had begun in 1965, dragged on. An antiwar movement had swept the country; still, about 58,000 Americans were killed and about 300,000 were wounded during the war. The Vietnam War, which finally came to an end in 1975, would become the longest war in U.S. history.

In 1974, Maris became eligible for induction into the National Baseball Hall of Fame. The Baseball Writers'

★ ★ ★ ★ ★

HANK AARON: BREAKING BABE RUTH'S RECORD

In the early 1970s, another of Babe Ruth's records seemed about to be broken. Hank Aaron of the Atlanta Braves was nearing the all-time career home-run record of 714 set by Babe Ruth. Aaron received the nickname "Hammerin' Hank" because of his ability to hammer out the home runs. He was born Henry Louis Aaron on February 5, 1934, in Mobile, Alabama. Like Roger Maris, Aaron played right field.

Aaron endured much of the same resentment toward breaking a record of Ruth's. Like Maris, Aaron received hate mail. The press followed Aaron's every move and demanded interviews. Aaron also had to overcome prejudice from those fans who did not want to see a black man beat Ruth's all-time home-run record. A few extreme racists sent Aaron death threats. The pressure on him was intense.

Aaron persevered, however, and on April 4, 1974, he tied Ruth's mark of 714 with a three-run homer off Jack Billingham of

Association of America (BBWAA) elects the players to the Hall of Fame; Maris would be eligible for consideration for the next 15 years. He needed more than 75 percent of the votes to qualify. He never received that total. The highest percentage that Maris tallied was about 42 percent. Maris told reporters he would consider it a great honor to be named to the Hall of Fame, but he was not expecting it to happen.

Around this time, in the mid-1970s, Maris quit smoking. He had been a heavy, three-pack-a-day smoker for many years. He had done advertising campaigns for cigarettes back in the 1960s. Maris knew now, however, that smoking was bad for his health. Once he stopped smoking, he quickly put on a great

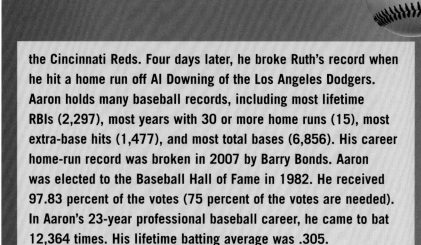

★ ★ ★ ★ ★ ★

the Cincinnati Reds. Four days later, he broke Ruth's record when he hit a home run off Al Downing of the Los Angeles Dodgers. Aaron holds many baseball records, including most lifetime RBIs (2,297), most years with 30 or more home runs (15), most extra-base hits (1,477), and most total bases (6,856). His career home-run record was broken in 2007 by Barry Bonds. Aaron was elected to the Baseball Hall of Fame in 1982. He received 97.83 percent of the votes (75 percent of the votes are needed). In Aaron's 23-year professional baseball career, he came to bat 12,364 times. His lifetime batting average was .305.

In 1990, Aaron's autobiography, *I Had a Hammer*, was released. In 1999, 25 years after Aaron broke Ruth's home-run record, Major League Baseball unveiled a new award, the Hank Aaron Award, given annually to the best overall hitter in each league. Not long after, in 2002, Aaron was honored with the Presidential Medal of Freedom.

deal of weight. He tried to stay active to control his weight and improve his health.

One way Maris liked to be active was to play golf. His sons enjoyed golf, and they all spent many hours on the course. In addition, Maris played in charity golf tournaments. Over a 10-year stretch, from 1974 to 1984, Maris played around 25 golf tournaments every year. In 1979, Roger and Pat even moved about 30 miles (48 kilometers) away from Gainesville into a house adjacent to a golf course. Maris loved the easy access to one of his favorite hobbies. He also took up fishing, after his boys introduced him to the sport. Maris had always been an outdoorsy person. Fishing allowed him to slow down and take in his surroundings.

The beer distributorship was running smoothly. As it took less of his attention, Maris spent his time watching his children participate in sports like baseball and basketball. He worked on cars and motorcycles with his sons. He took time with each of his kids to listen to their ideas and ambitions. He respected each of them as individual people and felt a close bond with all six.

Maris briefly returned to baseball when he became a hitting instructor to John Mayberry of the Kansas City Royals. The Royals wanted Maris to help Mayberry, a left-handed home-run hitter, perfect his swing. Maris enjoyed teaching in Fort Myers, Florida, and found Mayberry to be a responsive student.

VISITING STADIUMS PAST

On April 13, 1978, Maris did something he had put off doing for years. He entered Yankee Stadium. Since his retirement, the New York Yankees had asked Maris to come back on numerous occasions, but Maris had had no desire to go back. He had been through so much with the press and the booing fans that he simply wanted to stay away. He was happy to go about his business in Florida and leave the New York memories behind him.

The M&M Boys, Roger Maris and Mickey Mantle—now with a few more years under their belts—saluted the cheering fans during Opening Day ceremonies at Yankee Stadium in 1978. The appearance was Roger Maris's first at Yankee Stadium since he had been traded from the team after the 1966 season.

On this day, however, Maris was in the stadium for the Yankees' home opener. George Steinbrenner, the owner of the Yankees, had asked Maris and Mickey Mantle to participate in a flag-raising ceremony to start the new season. Maris agreed to participate if Steinbrenner gave the Oak Hill Private School in Gainesville, Florida, new sod and lights—and kept Maris's name out of the papers. Steinbrenner agreed.

There were 44,667 people in attendance for the game. The Yankees had not told the press about Maris's appearance, because they did not want him met with an onslaught of reporters. Maris's presence, therefore, was a surprise to the crowd. Once the fans recognized Roger Maris and Mickey Mantle walking onto the field, there was overwhelming cheering and a standing ovation, very different from the noises Maris had become used to hearing after 1961 in the same stadium.

Maris also made time to revisit Fargo, North Dakota, when he could. He and Pat still considered Fargo their hometown, and they felt a strong tie with the city. They had many friends with whom they stayed in touch over the years and liked to visit. Maris enjoyed watching the 1983 American Legion Baseball World Series in Fargo. It had been a long time since Maris had played for the American Legion. Instead of playing at Barnett Field, as he had, the '83 players were playing at the new Jack Williams Stadium.

A NEW BATTLE

In the fall of 1983, Maris found himself battling with health issues once again. This time, he could not stop what seemed to be ongoing colds and flu. He made an appointment to see a doctor, thinking that perhaps he was having sinus trouble. The doctor examined Maris and noticed that he had swollen lymph glands. The doctor ordered more tests. Upon looking over the test results, Maris's doctor diagnosed cancer of the lymph glands. The cancer had gone undetected for five years. Maris visited other doctors, but the results were always the same: He had cancer, and the cause was his heavy smoking habit years before. The good news, however, was that his kind of cancer had an 80 percent cure rate. Maris began chemotherapy in November. He was very sick, but the chemotherapy he received helped put the cancer in remission by April 1984. He felt optimistic and hopeful about his future.

Around this time, Jim McLaughlin and Bob Smith, two American Legion officials, spoke to Maris about opening a museum filled with Roger Maris memorabilia. (McLaughlin and Smith would not find out about Maris's cancer until later in the year.) Maris was hesitant at first. He wanted to ensure that the museum was attractive, proper, easy to get to, and secure. Maris donated nearly everything he owned to the museum, including scorecards, photographs, awards, bats, and balls. The few items he kept were his 1960 and 1961 Most Valuable Player plaques and his three World Series rings. The museum opened on June 23, 1984, in the West Acres Shopping Center in Fargo, North Dakota. Two-thousand people attended the opening.

McLaughlin had worked hard to ensure the authenticity of every item displayed in the museum. When he discovered that the New York Yankees had sent a No. 9 uniform made out of a material that was not used during Maris's day, he sent it back. The Yankees replaced it with an authentic uniform made of the heavy wool that Maris had worn. Andy Strasberg donated his Roger Maris baseball cards and a ticket stub from the game in which Maris hit his sixty-first home run in 1961.

Two days after the museum's opening, Maris was the host of the first Roger Maris-Shanley Open golf tournament. The tournament would raise money to help support Maris's former school, Shanley High School. The benefit dinner and golf tournament brought many professional baseball players and other entertainers, like Mickey Mantle, Whitey Ford, Bill Skowron, and Bob Allison. Now known as the Roger Maris Celebrity Benefit Golf Tournament, the event is still held each year. In 2007, participants included Minnesota Vikings quarterback Brooks Bollinger; former football star Lou Cordileone; former baseball stars Juan Berenguer, Rick Helling, Dave Kingman, and Tom Tresh; and Maris's number-one fan, Andy Strasberg. The tournaments have raised more than $1 million for charities such as the Roger Maris Cancer Center.

In July 1984, the New York Yankees retired Roger Maris's number: 9. With him at the ceremony was Arlene Howard, the widow of Elston Howard, whose number was also retired that day. Maris was unsure of the reception he would receive, so he appreciated the long and rousing ovation the crowd at Yankee Stadium gave him.

RETURNING TO "THE HOUSE THAT RUTH BUILT"

On July 21, 1984, the New York Yankees invited Maris to return to Yankee Stadium once again. At Old Timers' Day, the club planned to honor Maris with a plaque. In a special ceremony, they would then retire his number: 9. Maris was touched that the Yankees planned this homage for him. The plaque pays tribute to Maris's achievements at Yankee Stadium.

On the day of the ceremony, 250 fans from Fargo enjoyed seats behind home plate. Pat and all six children came to see Maris. He was unsure how New York fans would receive him in The House That Ruth Built. Maris worried about people booing him at the ceremony. Instead, Maris was welcomed with a long, standing ovation of cheers and applause. Maris felt appreciated and acknowledged. It was a long-awaited but happy moment in Maris's life. It made him proud to see his plaque hanging alongside those honoring other baseball greats, like Joe DiMaggio, Mickey Mantle, Casey Stengel, and Thurman Munson. This recognition meant more to Maris than any previous award. After years of harboring unpleasant feelings toward the Yankees, Maris felt at peace.

Maris returned to Yankee Stadium in April 1985 to receive the Lou Gehrig Pride of the Yankees award. Later in the spring, he came to New York to visit Dr. Ezra Greenson, a cancer specialist at Mount Sinai Hospital. Soon after that visit, Maris's cancer re-emerged. He was too sick to make an appearance at the 1985 Roger Maris Celebrity Benefit Golf Tournament in Fargo. His sons—Roger, Kevin, Randy, and Richard—did attend. Roger Jr. spoke at the dinner of his father's seriously weakened condition but noted that he had recently been feeling better.

Against
All Odds

During the last three months of Roger Maris's life, he was in a great deal of pain. He knew he was dying, but he accepted that and was thankful and happy to have his loving family by his side. In November 1985, Dr. Robert Oldham, a cancer researcher, announced that Maris had agreed to an experimental treatment. The treatment consisted of injecting part of Maris's cancerous tumor into a laboratory mouse. When the mouse had produced antibodies to counteract the tumor, technicians would extract the antibodies from the mouse and inject those antibodies into Maris. This kind of treatment had worked on patients when they had nine months to one year to allow the antibodies to work. Maris did not have that time.

After a two-year battle with lymphatic cancer, Roger Maris passed away on December 14, 1985, just a month after starting the experimental treatment. He died at M.D. Anderson Hospital and Tumor Institute in Houston, Texas. He was unable to have any visitors other than his immediate family during his last couple of days, because of the severity of his condition. Pat and the children were by his bed when he slipped into a coma and died. Maris was only 51 years old.

SAYING GOODBYE

Pat Maris oversaw the funeral arrangements. First, visitors could pay their respects on December 18 at an open-casket visitation at Boulger Funeral Home and St. Mary's Cathedral in Fargo. In the evening, visitors could gather for an hour-long prayer service at St. Mary's Cathedral. Five-hundred people attended.

The next day, Maris was buried at Holy Cross Catholic Cemetery in Fargo. During the funeral Mass beforehand, Pat, Susan, Roger Jr., Kevin, Randy, Richard, and Sandra stood together, giving one another support on this sad day. Roger's mother, father, and brother also mourned his death at the funeral. Twelve pallbearers—six former teammates and six personal friends—carried Maris's oak casket: Mickey Mantle, Clete Boyer, Bill Skowron, Whitey Ford, Mike Shannon, Whitey Herzog, Bob Allison, Dr. George Surprise, Big Julie Isaacson, Don Gooselaw, Dick Savageau, and Bob Wood. Around 1,000 mourners came to the funeral—800 people sat in the pews, 100 lined the inside walls of the church, and 100 watched the services in a basement room via closed-circuit television. Former Yankee teammates Bob Cerv, Ryne Duren, Bobby Richardson, and John Blanchard were among those sitting in the pews. Andy Strasberg, Maris's biggest baseball fan, flew to North Dakota from San Diego to be at the funeral and offer his support to the family.

On December 23, 1985, close to 3,000 people gathered in and around St. Patrick's Cathedral in New York City. George

Steinbrenner had organized the requiem services in memory of Roger Maris.

Guests included Pat Maris and her six children, former President Richard M. Nixon, New York City Mayor Edward I. Koch, U.S. Attorney Rudolph Giuliani, and former Yankee Yogi Berra. Roger Maris Jr. spoke to the congregation, and Susan, Kevin, Randy, Richard, and Sandra took part in the Offertory Procession. Opera singer Robert Merrill sang "The Lord's Prayer." At the end of the services, His Eminence John Cardinal O'Connor asked for one last burst of applause to honor Maris. The people rose to their feet, and a great applause rang out, lasting nearly a minute.

Pat Maris designed a diamond-shaped, gray-black head-stone with an image of Roger swinging left-handed and a caption reading "61, '61." The base of the tombstone reads "Against All Odds." She had the marker placed at his gravesite in time for Memorial Day in 1986.

MARIS'S HOME-RUN RECORD

In 1991, baseball commissioner Fay Vincent restored Roger Maris's name as the sole and official record holder of the most home runs in a season. In 1992, Maris again became eligible for induction into the National Baseball Hall of Fame through the Hall of Fame Committee on Baseball Veterans. He did not get enough votes. Although Maris is not in the Hall of Fame at this time, he is not altogether overlooked at the National Base-ball Hall of Fame Museum. His ball and bat from his record-breaking sixty-first home run are on display there.

Roger Maris's single-season home-run record held for 37 years. Then, in 1998, Mark McGwire of the St. Louis Cardinals and Sammy Sosa of the Chicago Cubs broke his season mark of 61 home runs. McGwire hit an impressive 70 home runs, and Sosa hit 66 during the season. Like Maris and Mantle, McGwire and Sosa were good friends who found themselves in the run-ning to break a record.

St. Louis Cardinals slugger Mark McGwire hugged Richard Maris, one of Roger Maris's sons, after McGwire hit his sixty-second home run of the 1998 season to break Roger Maris's 1961 record. At left is Roger Maris Jr.

When McGwire hit his sixty-second home run on September 8 at Busch Stadium in St. Louis, the Maris family was in the stands. McGwire ran over to Rich Maris and gave him a hug. As a tribute to Roger Maris, McGwire's foundation sends the Roger Maris Celebrity Benefit Golf Tournament a check every year for $6,200 to represent the one home run McGwire hit past Maris's sixty-first.

*61** THE MOVIE

Sports fans around the world will remember Roger Maris. Thanks to the efforts of actor Billy Crystal, who is a huge New York Yankees fan, others will get a chance to learn about Maris's story, too. Crystal grew up watching Roger Maris and Mickey Mantle. He saw the summer of '61 firsthand. He jumped at the chance to tell the world about this exciting time in history through a movie.

The head of HBO Sports, Ross Greenburg, contacted Crystal to ask him to produce a movie about the summer of '61 with him. The race to break Babe Ruth's record had left a memorable and lasting impression on Crystal. Crystal had had the opportunity to meet Mantle when both men appeared on *The Dinah Shore Show.* As a young boy, Crystal had idolized Mantle. After meeting him in person, the two went on to become good friends. Over the years, Crystal also became a close family friend of the Marises. Crystal had shared stories with both families. He knew this was the opportunity of a lifetime.

Hank Steinberg wrote the script for *61** alongside Crystal. Although initially Pat Maris was not the narrator of the story, Crystal suggested it be done that way. He knew how close Pat was to her husband, and Crystal felt that the bond between the two would add another dimension to the film. He thought that the movie was more than about a race—it was a story about losing a husband and a father.

Steinberg and Crystal spent long hours researching the film, as authenticity was of great importance to Crystal. They spent nearly two years developing the script before it went into production. Crystal hired C.J. Maguire, an experienced prop designer, and Rusty Smith, a trusted production designer, to help him create the feel he was after.

To portray Roger Maris, Crystal cast Barry Pepper, and to portray Mickey Mantle, he cast Thomas Jane. Pepper and Jane both put their trust into Crystal's knowledge of the Yankees,

Attending a screening of *61** in Los Angeles in April 2001 were *(from left)* Susan and Kevin Maris, two of Roger Maris's children, and Barry Pepper, who played Roger Maris in the HBO film. The movie portrayed the home-run race between Maris and Mickey Mantle during the 1961 season.

and both actors put much effort and time into their roles. Before filming, Pepper and Jane attended a baseball camp with Reggie Smith, a former Red Sox and Dodger player. Jane, who had never played baseball, not only had to learn to hit, but he had to learn to hit from both sides of the plate, as Mantle was a switch-hitter. Pepper, on the other hand, had to learn to hit from the left side of the plate like Maris. Pepper is right-handed so it took a lot of practice. Smith coached both players and helped them learn all the individual nuances and personal habits of Maris and Mantle.

The shooting schedule for *61** was tight—the movie was shot in 36 days. Some scenes were shot in the Los Angeles Coliseum, which was made to look like many different stadiums, from Baltimore's Memorial Stadium to Boston's Fenway Park. Tiger Stadium was also used to shoot scenes set in Tiger Stadium as well as those set in Yankee Stadium. To transform Tiger Stadium (which was no longer in use because the team had just built a new stadium) into Yankee Stadium, set designers matched the pale, mint-green color

★ ★ ★ ★ ★ ☆

THE ROGER MARIS MUSEUM

Jim McLaughlin and Bob Smith came up with the idea of creating a Roger Maris Museum. Once Maris was on board with the idea, he donated a wealth of artifacts and memorabilia to the museum, which is in the West Acres Shopping Center, a mall in Fargo, North Dakota. The museum opened its doors on June 23, 1984.

In 2003, West Acres completely rebuilt the museum. Visitors can sit in a video room on Yankee Stadium seats preserved from the time when Maris played there. They can watch numerous videos about Maris. The museum also includes replicas of Maris's Yankee locker from 1961 and his Yankee Stadium plaque. Visitors can see Maris's four major-league uniforms: those of the Cleveland Indians, the Kansas City Athletics, the New York Yankees, and the St. Louis Cardinals.

McLaughlin—along with Maris's wife, Pat, family, and special guests—attended a re-dedication when the new museum opened. The new museum better preserves and displays Maris's artifacts with improved glass, lighting, and ventilation. The museum allows baseball fans to learn about Maris through his large collection of memorabilia and informative descriptions.

of the original Yankee Stadium seats to an actual seat that Crystal had in his baseball memorabilia collection. It was a perfect match.

When the entire Maris family came to the screening of the movie, they loved it. After the screening, the family saw showings of the film in New York and Los Angeles. Pat Maris and Roger Maris Jr. saw it with President George W. Bush at the White House. Pat and the Maris children thought *61** portrayed Roger Maris fairly and honestly. It showed his many sides: a great ballplayer, a loving father, and a private man. Maris struggled with the relentlessness of the press and their repetitive questions; he struggled with injuries and illnesses. But his generous nature and his strong-willed patience and endurance saw him through—and he triumphed. The film was first shown on HBO in April 2001.

A BASEBALL LEGEND

Roger Maris believed in honesty and integrity. He believed in saying what was on his mind. He did not like sugar-coating; instead, he told it as he saw it. He did not pretend to be someone he was not.

Maris was a doting father, a loving husband, and an incredible baseball player. His natural speed, strength, power, and agility enabled him to excel as a top athlete. Some people thought that Maris was one of baseball's all-time greatest outfielders. They also recognized him to be an aggressive base runner and a powerful batter. He knew how to best help his team win games—he could run extra bases, bunt, or throw a man out at home plate from right field. Those natural instincts were a part of what made Maris an outstanding player.

Some sports critics say that Maris was a one-year wonder. Maris did have an especially strong year in 1961; it was a great feat to break the single-season home-run record. Hitting 61 home runs in a season when the fans were cheering for someone else must have been mentally, emotionally, and

Roger Maris may be best known for his record-breaking season in 1961. Here, Yogi Berra congratulates Maris after he hit a home run in late September that year. Yet, Maris's speed around the bases and terrific fielding skills should also be remembered, as should his actions off the field.

physically exhausting. Yet Maris accomplished a great deal in other years, as well. He appeared in All-Star Games in 1959, 1960, 1961, and 1962. He won the Sultan of Swat Award in two straight years: 1960 and 1961. He helped his ball club get to the World Series seven times: 1960, 1961, 1962, 1963, 1964, 1967, and 1968. He was named the Most Valuable Player in the American League for two consecutive years: 1960 and 1961.

Maris placed the utmost importance on being a good citizen. He wanted to treat the people around him fairly, and he wanted to be treated fairly in return. Maris almost never talked poorly of the many New York reporters who wrote unfavorably about him. Maris did not fight back against the fans who threw items at him in right field and shouted insults from the stands. He did not gloat after hitting a home run. He did not party into the small hours of the morning after a winning game. That was not who Maris was.

Roger Maris was a private man. He enjoyed playing baseball because it encompassed aspects of life that he so loved—being outdoors, competing, pushing his body to extremes. He also loved his life off the field. Pat and his six children made Maris's world complete. With his family and close friends, Maris could be himself. He could joke around, sit and talk, work on house projects, and take part in barbecues and dinner parties. He could toss a ball around with his children in the backyard, go on hunting and fishing trips, and play golf. Maris lived his life the way he wanted to—with privacy and by doing what he believed to be right.

STATISTICS

ROGER MARIS
Primary position: Right field (Also CF)

Full name: Roger Eugene Maras
Born: September 10, 1934, Hibbing, Minnesota
Died: December 14, 1985, Houston, Texas •
Height: 6'0" • Weight: 204 lbs. • Teams:
Cleveland Indians (1957–1958); Kansas City
Athletics (1958–1959); New York Yankees
(1960–1966); St. Louis Cardinals (1967–1968)

YEAR	TEAM	G	AB	H	HR	RBI	BA
1957	CLE	116	358	84	14	51	.235
1958	CLE/KCA	150	583	140	28	80	.240
1959	KCA	122	433	118	16	72	.273
1960	NYY	136	499	141	39	112	.283
1961	NYY	161	590	159	61	142	.269
1962	NYY	157	590	151	33	100	.256
1963	NYY	90	312	84	23	53	.269
1964	NYY	141	513	144	26	71	.281
1965	NYY	46	155	37	8	27	.239
1966	NYY	119	348	81	13	43	.233
1967	STL	125	410	107	9	55	.261
1968	STL	100	310	79	5	45	.255
TOTAL		1,463	5,101	1,325	275	851	.260

KEY: CLE = Cleveland Indians; KCA = Kansas City Athletics; NYY = New York Yankees;
STL = St. Louis Cardinals; G = Games; AB = At-bats; H = Hits; HR = Home runs;
RBI = Runs batted in; BA = Batting average

CHRONOLOGY

1934 September 10: Born Roger Eugene Maras in Hibbing, Minnesota.

1949 Begins to play American Legion baseball in Fargo, North Dakota.

1952 Graduates from Shanley High School in Fargo.

1953 Signs contract with the Cleveland Indians; plays for their Class C farm team, the Fargo-Moorhead Twins.

1954 Plays for Keokuk in the Class B Three-I League.

1955 Plays for Tulsa of the Class AA Texas League and Reading of the Class AA Eastern League.

1956 Plays for the Indianapolis Indians of the Class AAA American Association; marries Patricia Carvell on October 13.

1957 Makes major-league debut with the Cleveland Indians.

1958 June 15: Traded to the Kansas City Athletics.

1959 December 11: Traded to the New York Yankees.

1960 Named the American League Most Valuable Player; wins the Gold Glove Award and the Sultan of Swat Award.

1961 October 1: Hits his sixty-first home run of the season to break Babe Ruth's single-season home-run record.

Named the American League Most Valuable Player; wins the Sultan of Swat Award and the Hickok Belt.

1965   June 20: Breaks bone in right hand while sliding into home plate.

1966   December 8: Traded to the St. Louis Cardinals.

1968   August 5: Announces that he will retire at the end of the season.

1978   April 13: Returns to Yankee Stadium for the first time since his trade from the team.

1983   Diagnosed with cancer of the lymph glands.

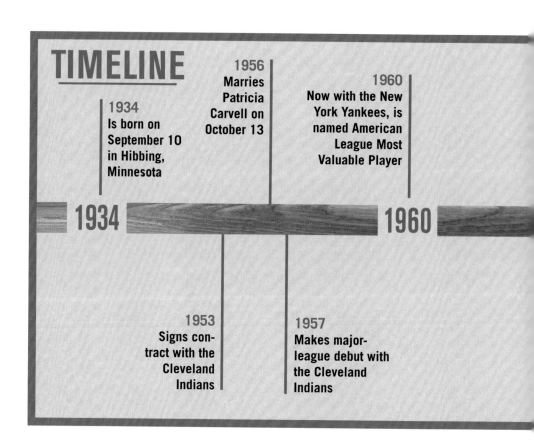

TIMELINE

1956
Marries Patricia Carvell on October 13

1934
Is born on September 10 in Hibbing, Minnesota

1960
Now with the New York Yankees, is named American League Most Valuable Player

1934   1960

1953
Signs contract with the Cleveland Indians

1957
Makes major-league debut with the Cleveland Indians

1984   **June 23:** The Roger Maris Museum opens in Fargo, North Dakota.

June 25: The first Roger Maris-Shanley Open golf tournament is held.

July 21: The New York Yankees retire his number: 9.

1985   **December 14:** Dies from lymphatic cancer in Houston, Texas, at age 51.

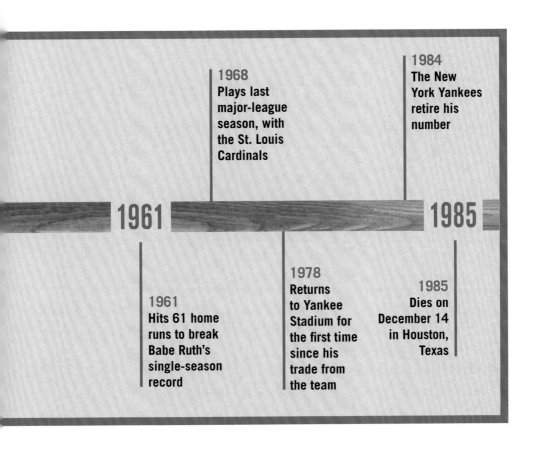

1968
Plays last major-league season, with the St. Louis Cardinals

1984
The New York Yankees retire his number

1961

1985

1961
Hits 61 home runs to break Babe Ruth's single-season record

1978
Returns to Yankee Stadium for the first time since his trade from the team

1985
Dies on December 14 in Houston, Texas

GLOSSARY

at-bat   An official turn at batting that is charged to a base-ball player, except when the player walks, sacrifices, is hit by a pitched ball, or is interfered with by a catcher. At-bats are used to calculate a player's batting average and slugging percentage.

ball   A pitch that does not pass over home plate in the strike zone. A batter who receives four balls gets a walk.

baseball commissioner   The highest-ranking office in Major League Baseball.

batting average   The number of hits a batter gets divided by the number of times the player is at bat. For example, 3 hits in 10 at-bats would be a .300 batting average.

bunt   A ball hit softly so that it rolls to a particular spot in the infield. A bunt is usually hit by holding the bat loosely and letting the ball bounce off it rather than swinging the bat.

chemotherapy   The use of chemical agents in the treatment or control of disease—as in cancer.

curveball   A pitch that curves on its way to the plate, thanks to the spin a pitcher places on the ball when throwing. Also known as a "breaking ball."

disabled list   In Major League Baseball, the disabled list is a way for teams to remove injured players from their rosters. Other players can be called up as replacements during this time.

doubleheader   Two baseball games played by the same teams on the same day.

exhibition game   A game that does not count in the season's final standings.

farm team   A team that provides training and experience for young players, with the expectation that successful players will move to the major leagues.

fastball   A pitch that is thrown so that it has maximum speed. It can be gripped in any number of ways, most commonly touching two baseball seams (a two-seamer) with the index finger and middle finger, or across four seams (a four-seamer).

grand slam   A home run that is hit when the bases are loaded.

hamstring muscle   Any of three muscles at the back of the thigh that function to flex and rotate the leg and extend the thigh.

home run   When a batter hits a ball into the stands in fair territory, it is a home run. The batter may also hit an inside-the-park home run if the ball never leaves the playing field and the runner is able to reach home plate without stopping before being tagged by a defensive player. A home run counts as one run, and if there are any runners on base when a home run is hit, they too score.

knuckleball   A slow pitch that is thrown with little spin by gripping the ball with the knuckles or the tips of the fingers. The pitch moves erratically and unpredictably.

lineup   A list that is presented to the umpire and opposing coach before the start of the game that contains the order in which the batters will bat as well as the defensive fielding positions they will play.

line drive   A batted ball, usually hit hard, that never gets too far off the ground. Typically a line drive will get beyond the infield without touching the ground or will be hit directly at a player and be caught before it touches the ground.

MVP   The Most Valuable Player award (commonly known as the MVP) is an annual award given to one outstanding player in each league (American and National) of Major League Baseball.

pennant   The title in the American League and National League. In Roger Maris's day, the pennant went to the first-place team in each league. Today, each league has two rounds of play-offs, with the champion earning the pennant. The two pennant winners meet in the World Series.

pull the ball   To hit the ball hard with a full swing toward the natural side of the field. A right-handed hitter pulls the ball to the left side of the field; a left-handed batter, to the right side.

RBI   A run (or runs) batted in is generally given to a batter for each run scored as the result of his appearance at the plate.

rookie   A player who is playing his first season on a professional team.

scout   A person who seeks undiscovered talent, such as a baseball player, to sign to a professional contract.

spring training   A period of practice and exhibition games in professional baseball that begins in late winter and goes until the start of the season in spring.

stolen base   When a runner successfully advances to the next base while the pitcher is delivering a pitch.

strike   A pitch that is swung at and missed or a pitch that is in the strike zone and is not swung at. Three strikes and the batter is out.

strike zone   The area directly over home plate up to the batter's chest (roughly where the batter's uniform lettering is) and down to his or her knees. Different umpires have slightly different strike zones, and players only ask that they be consistent.

sweep   To win every game in a tournament or series.

switch-hit   To hit from both sides of the plate—right-handed and left-handed.

umpire   The official who rules on plays. For most baseball games, a home-plate umpire calls ball and strikes, and other umpires in the infield rule on outs at bases.

walk   When a batter takes four pitches out of the strike zone, the batter receives a walk, also called a base on balls, and is awarded first base.

World Series   The championship series of Major League Baseball. The Series is played between the pennant winners of the American League and the National League in a best-of-seven play-off.

BIBLIOGRAPHY

Bingham, Walter. "Double M for Murder: Maris and Mantle Are the Bludgeons That May Bring the Pennant Back to New York." *Sports Illustrated.* July 4, 1960.

Dahlberg, Tim, "North Dakota Seeks Justice for Maris." *Boston Globe.* April 3, 2005. Available online at http://www.boston .com/sports/baseball/articles/2005/04/03/n_dakota_seeks_ justice_for_maris/.

Elrick, Ted. "Billy Crystal's 61." *DGA Monthly.* Available online at http://www.dga.org/news/v26_1/feat_billycrystals61.php3.

Grossfeld, Stan. "Hall of Injustice?" *Boston Globe.* February 4, 2005. Available online at http://www.boston.com/sports/ baseball/articles/2005/02/04/hall_of_injustice?pg=full.

James, Bill. *The Bill James Historical Baseball Abstract.* New York: Villard Books, 1988.

Persaud, Babita. "A Slugger's Story." *St. Petersburg Times.* April 26, 2001. Available online at http://www.sptimes.com/ News/042601/TampaBay/A_slugger_s_story_.shtml.

Reston, James. "The Asterisk that Shook the Baseball World." *New York Times.* October 1, 1961.

Rosenfeld, Harvey. *Still a Legend: The Story of Roger Maris.* Lincoln, Neb.: iUniverse Inc., 1991.

Strasberg, Andy. "Roger Maris and Me." *Chicken Soup for the Soul.* 2000. Available online at http://www.chickensoup.com/ stories/baseball_fans/Roger_Maris_and_Me.htm.

FILM
61*, 2001 (television, DVD)

WEB SITES
American Legion Baseball. Available online at http://www.baseball.legion.org. Sections used: "Rules and Forms" and "History."

Baseball Almanac. Available online at http://www.baseball-almanac.com.

BaseballLibrary.com: The Home of Baseball History. Available online at http://www.baseballlibrary.com. Sections used: "Ballplayers" and "Teams."

The Baseball Page. Available online at http://www.thebaseballpage.com.

Baseball Reference. Available online at http://www.baseball-reference.com.

Fargo, North Dakota: Its History and Images. Available online at http://www.fargo-history.com.

MeritCare. Available online at http://www.meritcare.com.

The National Baseball Hall of Fame and Museum. Available online at http://www.baseballhalloffame.org. Sections used: "The Hall of Famers," "The Museum," "News."

The Official Roger Maris Web Site. Available online at http://www.rogermaris.com. Sections used: "Biography," "Career Statistics," "Photos," and "Baseball Cards."

The Official Site of Major League Baseball. Available online at http://mlb.mlb.com/index.jsp. Section used: "News—History."

The Official Site of Minor League Baseball. Available online at http://www.minorleaguebaseball.com. Section used: "History."

The Official Site of the New York Yankees. Available online at http://newyork.yankees.mlb.com. Sections used: "Team History" and "About Yankee Stadium."

The Official Web Site of the Sultan of Swat. Available online at http://www.baberuth.com. Sections used: "About Babe Ruth," "Biography," "Achievements," "Quotes, and "Fast Facts."

Roger Maris Celebrity Benefit Golf Tournament. Available online at http://www.rogermarisgolf.com. Sections used: "History," "Information," "News Releases," and "Cover Stories."

Roger Maris Museum. Available online at http://www.rogermarismuseum.com. Sections used: "Museum," "Memories," "Stats," "Early Years," and "Getting Here."

FURTHER READING

BOOKS

Gutman, Bill. *It's Outta Here! The History of the Home Run from Babe Ruth to Barry Bonds.* Dallas, Texas: Taylor Publishing Company, 2005.

MacKay, Claire. *Touching All the Bases: Baseball for Kids of All Ages.* Tonawanda, N.Y.: Firefly Books Ltd., 1996.

Mantle, Mickey with Herb Gluck. *The Mick.* New York: Doubleday, 1985.

Mintzer, Rich. *The Everything Kids' Baseball Book.* Cincinnati: Adams Media Group, 2004.

Rosenfeld, Harvey. *Still a Legend: The Story of Roger Maris.* Lincoln, Neb.: iUniverse Inc., 1991.

Smith, Ron and Billy Crystal. *61*: The Story of Roger Maris, Mickey Mantle and One Magical Summer.* New York: McGraw Hill, 2001.

Stout, Glenn. *Yankees Century: 100 Years of New York Yankees Baseball.* Boston: Houghton Mifflin, 2002.

WEB SITES

Baseball Almanac
http://www.baseball-almanac.com

Baseball Reference
http://www.baseball-reference.com

The Official Roger Maris Web Site
http://www.rogermaris.com

The Official Site of Major League Baseball
http://mlb.mlb.com

The Official Site of the New York Yankees
http://newyork.yankees.mlb.com

Roger Maris Museum
http://www.rogermarismuseum.com

PICTURE CREDITS

INDEX

ABOUT THE AUTHOR

ANNE M. TODD received a bachelor of arts degree in English and American Indian studies from the University of Minnesota. She has written 20 nonfiction children's books, including biographies on American Indians, political leaders, and entertainers. Todd is also the author of the following Chelsea House books: *Hamid Karzai* from the Modern World Leaders series, *Mohandas Gandhi* from the Spiritual Leaders and Thinkers series, *Chris Rock* from the Black Americans of Achievement Legacy Edition series, and *Vera Wang* from the Asian Americans of Achievement series. She lives in Prior Lake, Minnesota, with her husband, Sean, and three sons, Spencer, William, and Henry.